TYRANNY
AND THE DEVIL

Richard Chaffer

To Sherma,
for believing in me.

Oh as I was young and easy in the mercy of his means,
Time held me green and dying
Though I sang in my chains like the sea.

—Dylan Thomas

Tyranny and the Devil
Copyright © 2009 by Richard Chaffer

Cover design by LeFroste exclusively for
EOD by graphic artist Giovanni Duenas
Library of Congress
Cataloging-in-Publishing Data
Chaffer, Richard (1952-)
Printed in the United States of America

PART ONE

I

This nervous and choleric rant in which I find myself is my great misfortune. Add to this that my appetites and passions were few and you have a keen sense of my disposition. But what was more, I want to know, is this clamor of society surmountable? I seem to shudder for lack of tenderness and I am dwarfed in my affairs. I do not want 'them' to make of me the devil! Whomever 'they' are is laying in wait. What I want to say favorably upon this morning is that, at times, it is a stroke of good fortune biding my time with the errantry of the fantastic. However, equally so, do you see, it is tantamount to suicide as you will espy. My cunning is limitless though 'they' raise objections that are beyond reproach. Am I wasting time in my efforts to draw a bead on such subjects? The subject, that is, of pursuit and foul play.

What, in heaven's name, is there to drive away these curses and their suicidal mandates?

With what pose can one descry these ruins? Leave me alone where the river parts and you will find me ubiquitous and alive, the suitor of tall tales. And here, indeed, I must make amends, amends and metamorphoses where need be. The vicious wounds that I have received in my eternal struggle forces my present posture. Yes, I have suffered the buckram of a former diplomat but I wasn't entirely without laughter. However, would such old wounds fester? I have, after all, been through all matters of things. And, of course, incalculable are the risks of authorship. So here I sit as morose as winter's garden but as free as winter's rain. It is a liberation that isn't without pleasure and pain. So I must dust these cobwebs off it being such a lovely and glorious day. Today I shall not ask what hypotheses and philosophical rant with which to prepare myself. Instead we might do well to query the apartment's groundkeeper.

Is he one and the same as a soul-keeper? I swear to you his fathomless eyes are quite filled with tales. However, with his peculiar manners, I must ask from whom or where he is duly inspired.

His replies always perplex me. At one time he seems to say that we are nothing more than a spate of skeletal remains while, at other times, he will suggest that we live forever. With each encounter the curtains will rise and fall, the shutters will be drawn and withdrawn revealing only the portals of this battle that lay before us. At times there lay only snippets of vulgar discourse with which to parley while at still others there are voluminous accounts that beg your mind to reciprocate even if they be no more than expropriated themes.

Oh, but I have begun this little book from fragments and segmental prose to the original text that lay in the gutter. Now it is time to collect my thoughts and proceed with the substance of my story. I am in fear that I will stray from time to time, my status being desultory. What of this racket, the devil and din of distinction? I will, I must improvise only when I can go no further. But there are so many foul illustrations it is futile to acquiesce. It would seem that I only wince while others reconcile. At the sea today I must gain my composure in a sunset of hot ash. Later I will witness a

7

blast of wind that devours the horizon. But presently in the sharp light the brine is quite pungent. The pith of my reflections arrives from faraway in the shapeless high seas. In these traditions I will wade not without shedding tears and moaning for a place on earth to be renewed. As a reprieve to my troubles I soundlessly crept up the sinuous path. Yes, I was making great strides, transcending all barriers and so forth and so on. The hourglass was never before so patient. The waters seemed to hiss at the promontory. Was I learned, was I mad, what will be my testimony?

As for now I must return to land and seek comfort from kind words. Henceforth my ample bitterness is replaced by sweet patterns of thought. Thus no longer do the faces pass by so pathetically. After such a siege of memory what otherwise lay ragged was now lustrous in a limpid light. I sometimes feel, in fact, that I am gravid with a child of wisdom, a reproof to these hard times. But amongst this agony and anguish I must plant my feet and tear myself from the inimitable horror. For human misery lay everywhere and perhaps I was

8

atop the pile but nevertheless I was part of it. So I have wept on occasion. Was this nothing more than a manifestation of what others participate in day by day? I couldn't allow this expansive curiosity on my tail to trample me. It was meant, perhaps to be, only a good-natured nudge and not a source of horror. Enough of this sorrow and pity worth no more than a glimpse. I was merely riding out the inventions of an exquisite past time, snatching at the extraordinary and rejecting the execrable.

I must not lose confidence in myself and I must apologize for my poor habits. Namely the peculiarity of throwing a stone or two at my nemesis, thus granting them the respect they do not deserve. But I must insist that rumors contrary to myself must cease. Please, in this regard, ease my mind with this rather conventional wisdom; to linger where the consequences are not so ambiguous. Henceforth I will become disengaged from nature's dalliances and forego any acts of lunacy.

Yes, I must stand tall in word and deed escaping from all forms of maliciousness. All things considered it was an opportune time for me to shine. Nonetheless, is there anything about these words that is salvageable? If I might raise my muse I might make great strides, sometimes in tranquility, sometimes in the despair few have known.

The light like gold dust parades in front of my eyes. Timorous lays my soul these past few days. All but the slightest of eccentricities have been permitted to usurp my time in these glorious trials. Upon the threshold of delivering myself from these heady climes, I croon and sing. My protestations are few but they come without any hesitations on my part to derail them. Meanwhile this vacancy in my eyes is genuine and it issues from the desperation of all others. What is patent is what meets the eye. There is no need to disinter the depths for the superficial. They are one and the same. Oh, but the spleen of these words! It was enough to make you butt your head.

Across the street there stands a woman playing at catching the sunlight with her hands. But the blind was never so blind. Above me the clouds are red and the sky is blue. The summer light is beginning to pale. My faculties are spent. I do not know which way to turn. My sirens seemed to say, 'why, we are growing you up lad. 'Their tone is incisive, their substance acute. The veins of my thoughts are prodigious. I huddle in a corner of the bookstore to slink away from their grasp. Once again I must sacrifice exultation for the pedestrian and the woes of discontent. Nausea accompanies me.

I returned to my little room where my heart lay broken. I lie in bed unable to rise while the commotion outdoors is drawing in upon me. What tears speak the truth, I must ask, though there is no answer? Understand me, there is no way out. None! Like a man half-possessed I search for the tools of my trade, rummaging for any and all means with which to combat the narratives of these faint whisperings. However the stamp is upon me no matter what direction I blunder. I must confess my last installment to a publisher was a nasty bit of news. To the many rejections I say, so be it! "Yes," I shall say, "send me a' dreamin'!" For when darkness reigns and the bridge is far I keep a good work ethic close to me while I scour the countryside with much scrutiny and parsimony alike.

I can see that, by now, you doubt my veracity and my several terms. But were we not meant for each other? I must, like you, savor this life. At the same time I feel like a stylist at crime, though I am well aware that I haven't committed any such act. My mind has been ransacked but there was still an edge to it that precipitated caution.

Sitting on a park bench I took notice of a woman across from me. Her habit, it must be noted, was to open her eyes wide and then to close them briefly. It was akin to a glandular moment, committed involuntarily, and it spelled out definition with each look. Sitting there forlorn I began to ask myself if it wouldn't be wise to show my writings to somebody other than a publishing house. But to whom, I thought. Besides, for the most part, they were merely heavy-handed words destined for the incinerator. No, I must be clear-minded, I must struggle, for I am simply a word monger and a menace. When will I come into my own? A decent book, well, I would never pull it off. But in distinct detail I recall that which has befallen me. Should we or not commit these memories to a red letter day? But should I continue among these ashes? "Why, of course!" I muttered, "Such madness I have never known," I gurgled, and I fell into the laughter that had been missing for some time.

Today I find myself as high as heaven. A neighbor's child is dancing and her little hands are fluttering like sparrows. Yes, like little puppets they wave in the cool breeze. I am at home. What do you propose that I do? I have entitled a future book *Another Chance*. It is to be staged at a nightclub called 'the Meadows. 'How did I come to these crossroads? I know that you must be thinking 'that country gentleman, that man again! 'But I am not through yet. These others, pursuing me with devious means are not right. They are not entirely real and they are tailing me with severity and without restraint. My story shall be one of nature and humanity. The equation is set in blood. Its discovery, its harsh origins had brought me to my feet. I must be something more than a graveyard writer. Today the bustle is everywhere. There is no gainsaying it,

I must write as though I am at the height of my powers. I must edit each book with a razor. And I must try and try again until once and for all the pieces fit, and fit very handsomely.

II

What I would not do for a witness to this despotism! Must I join the bat society? I've had quite enough of its sound. I am determined that I shall rise even if I have to take a cudgel to these damned voices. But lo and behold, it is the era of ultrasound. The ringing in my ears has been fierce. By all appearances these trappings of ultrasound want to cozy up with me expressing erotomania, then suicide. But in the midst of these reflections I ask myself, what do you really wish to write? My mind is teeming with insults. However, were there not fire in these words I would soon surrender. Yes, the roots of evil run deep and I am in no mood for games, but games I am forced to play. I must confess that I shy away from all forms of confrontation. Oh, but to laugh or to cry! How long must I suffer their company? The slightest of noises is my sworn enemy. Today, for whatever reasons, the sky is opening up and there is a clearing in my mind. In this regard I must be strong. My heart says so. And there is, nonetheless, music to my suffering and sorrow.

Perhaps, with a little more time, I shall become a lyricist no matter how desperate the circumstances. But, believe me, the piteous circumstances are at rehearsal as I speak and I only wish to bow out. So you see, at times, my courage is on the wane. The voices rise up and there enters these braggarts. They are invariably a stones throw from any direction. As I have said sometimes I am as free as rain while at other times I can only struggle unsuccessfully at the commotion being waged against me. There is nothing more irksome than to cower before these fledglings. One day I will die but until then I must scribble. It is too bold and undeserving to wish for something other than this. What is invaluable is here in the moment, as they say. But am I becoming a victim of platitudes?

I am curious now about the previous tenant. What were their thoughts as they abided here? I can hear the cries in the street. Could he have interpreted them in the same way? They are filled with absolute madness and one hears them all of

2

the time. As night falls I will often indulge myself with a glass of wine. This is my few granules of sleep. In this period of time I will often effortlessly fill a page of sumptuous prose for which I pat myself soundly on the back. The next morning entirely appalled I will crush the paper and deposit it neatly into the waste basket. And I ask myself, with some amusement, what other pretty, little stories do we have in mind?

Last night it was so very cold that I slept with my socks and jacket on. I managed to rise and stoke a fire to take the chill off and I made eggs and toast to avoid going out for a meal among a crowd of people. People, I must say, that wouldn't give you the time of day. Afterwards I will take my constitutional, a brisk walk passed the vendors and shops of every imagining. I can easily hear the ultrasound crystals of a transducer and with this implement, this god-awful medium of insanity, I will roam with variable frequencies at my back. Oh, believe me, this pack of wolves will leave no stone unturned. Nevertheless, who is pushing the buttons I will never know. I am merely left to pontifi-

3

cate from my altar as all of these various recruits stream along the many escarpments.

At home I lay down, my barren one room nothing more than four bay windows and a bed. Tired but restless, my mind sought out a target of sorts with which to occupy time. I would count by denominations of fifteen every cluster of objects that my eyes fell upon. These objects made claim to my attention such that the numbers began to grow more and more abundant and with it my vexation grew as well. I would count out or multiply the numbers with increasing enthusiasm but an enthusiasm that fell quite short of conferring any satisfaction. Inextricably tied to this phenomenon were voices. Voices whose meaning wasn't decipherable but which, nonetheless, begged for attention and disrupted my game of numbers. Henceforth, I would mutter inanities and profanity to which I would rise to my feet declaring my premises off limits to these devils and demons. Toward those that I felt were watching me through the walls I acted as though I was suffering a heart attack. My object was to try vehemently to flush out

4

their secret lairs and hiding places. But without any success I became discouraged at these ploys and increasingly annoyed at their absolute secrecy.

At such times I would finally rifle through the debris of my brain realizing that this raving was slowly being displaced and with it there arose the revelation that I was not only not foreign to sorrow but that neither was I foreign to happiness. I quipped, "Sometimes one must leave his home to find his home." And I laughed reservedly, not wishing for 'them' to make too much of a mockery of me. In fact, from the hush of silence that ensued I believed that I had penetrated their thick pates with just the proper touch. So many times before I had tried against overwhelming odds to reach the summit but without consummation. Presently I waded in the full glory of this triumph. I stood erect, waving my arms to and fro, tears rolling down my cheeks, ecstatic, and yes, even noble in my cause. The cause, that is, that kept me swimming through these troubled times.

Following such activities often left me exhausted and I would find myself nestling up for a good snooze. Other times, I would find myself no more than a bundle of neuropathy cursing at 'them' not to hamper my progress. For I divined that there was no beginning and no end, only a continuum.

There is an ample stream near my home. Before nightfall, better yet, before night's end, the wind seems to rise and the waters flow more deeply. Though I am drawn to it I have only visited during morning and the afternoon hours. There I bask in the sun tutoring my wasted mind. I sing quietly from the throat, don't you know. I forget what ditties I have given rise to and it isn't mine to dwell upon it. It is only my obsessive dream that these voices get a new livelihood, but it falls upon deaf ears. They are as adamant as am I. After all they proceed as if they are my judge, jury, and executioner. Accordingly the consequences of my life have become enormous. With all of these travails I am digging myself deeper into the mire. But as I have said there is no definitive escape thus far. Will I die honorably or will I die with these voices intact? These are, indeed, desperate hours and

6

such cruelty is unforgivable. They will have no difficulty covering up my death. Nevertheless, toward this struggle I am convinced of my survival. I must persevere despite the exhaustive forms of mayhem. My sole conclusion is that I am the victim of experiments of sorts and while others seem to lie by omission I stick fast to the inventions that won't abandon me.

The evening stars beckon to me. The volume of light has subsided and these devils, nonetheless, are in my blood. Oh, this wretched, wretched world! There is no collaborating and my little room is my incarceration. Sometimes I curse my imaginings like I curse the sky. Other times I marvel above the ruins where it seems that the tiger stripes the horizon. There and then I repeat to myself that I must burn these letters, the letters of one who has been forsaken. Oh, but I can barely speak. I must name my nemesis! I must vanish such that I will never see you again. But first I must astound 'them' and that is that. Meanwhile the well has run dry. The chasms are great. The insults that I feel are genuine but so is the vehemence of my expression.

Perhaps one day I will no longer have to carry this torch. Yes, but I must astound them and make them all proud of me. Meanwhile this fucking horse of words has me chomping at the bit. I must leave this disease behind me if there be such an uncanny illness. One thing for certain is that it is essential, nay, it is paramount that I rise above these spirits of evil.

It is the morning after and my eyes are quite cloudy. I must go. My public is waiting. One might say "This damned witch hunt!" but the sirens are all about me. Shall I boast with vile language toward my captors? Mine is, after all, to waste not and to accommodate. It is clear that I belong neither here nor anywhere. But forgive me the shroud that I wear. I must pay my respects to my allies. Shall I throw myself at your feet or should I shout from the rooftops? I am not above such a feat as I am neither above superstition nor remorse. But for now I am saddled with these burdens. Remonstrations from the heart, one might say. Precious are my biddings and the delicacy of

8

these promptings. Sometimes audacious are my moods while cowardice is my reaction. The irrational has constituted my past and presently my public is crying out to the hilt. And I, I shall continue drifting until my heart breaks. Meanwhile I must burst into tears. You must see that I need a decisive conclusion and why not a book to ask for as much?

I walk to the bay window and peer out at the multitudes. I feel as though 'they' were all there for the asking. I feel like a prince or a king but I couldn't tell you why. Benevolence seems quite near and again my mood has swung around. I lay down and let my thoughts drift. Before my eyes lay titles of stories and poems. One after another arises without the least bit of trouble. I was dancing with these words and I was both moved and touched.

I reached for a pen and in this nervous and agitated state I began to scribble an outline to a short story and various snippets of poems. Perhaps I was onto something. It was perfectly clear that to face a day similar to today I must relinquish all cares. I must seize these words by the throat, if you will, and take my good work to these publishers that normally appeared so remote and unapproachable. Would those about me, the benevolent as well as the malicious, permit me to have one day of deliverance from self indulgence and anonymity? Would 'they' succumb to tolerance of these parables by my side? Perhaps there would be a little reward and some financial success. In the meantime the titles were coming and going. Such titles as: *The Mangroves*, The *Man Who Could Not Speak*, and *Dying Among the Vines*. If need be, I could pedal my writings from door to door.

Soon my meager inheritance would be gone and I would have to procure a mailbox at the post office. I would do well to purchase a sleeping bag and a mess kit for when I would undoubtedly become homeless. Perhaps at the stream by my present room I might encamp. Certainly I did not wish to run into the law and be jailed as a vagrant and vagabond. However, memory of once indulging my thoughts at this rivulet and dissuading me from the acid fury I was experiencing struck me the

10

wrong way. So I dismissed this notion. I might do well to move, I thought, but this town was much like the next. There were a handful of people who knew me by name. Yes, this agreed with me and, I suppose, I was inextricably bound here like it that much or not.

I rolled a cigarette and leaned back upon the lawn taking in the day. My eyes swept the horizon, trying to put my predicament in the proper frame. Others appeared desperate beneath the placid surface but nothing arose beyond it. There was simply a hollow cry. Nevertheless, it certainly was curious how these others were so quietly chained to one another. Anyway easy discourse had abandoned me. I swear that I could hear heckles and jeers among this feeble entourage. I poured through my notes with the same hunger that I had possessed a few hours before. Whatever I write I must hurry. It is with both eyes that I now see. Yes, I was head-strong and this much had kept me alive. On the other hand I was in no way saved from whimper-ing, if not outright copious tears. The efforts of all and sundry must be applauded even if it was done

11

surreptitiously. Whatever the score of events it was still the simple things to which we cling that mattered. Why frown upon it? We must play the cards we are dealt.

III

Weeks have passed and I have established an agenda that fits well with my constitution. Hunger is my biggest enemy. In this connection I've arranged the morning hours to write my poetry and short stories while in the afternoon I will collect countless bottles and cans for recycling. Writing is casually done at the library where I enjoy the hush that surrounds me as opposed to human traffic and the natural sounds from the stream. On top of this I nourish the quiet company where I can be seen and spoken to if the mood fits. I am discovering more and more that I lose my strength and identity when I am alone and invisible to the eyes of others.

Today I visited my mailbox and I was very surprised to retrieve a response to one of the poems I had sent to a magazine. This whetted my enthusiasm until I realized upon reading further that they wanted for me to pay for my publication. Imagine that! According to them I was a rare talent, the editor's choice, destined for great things, and so on and so forth. For only the pittance of fifty dollars I could possess a finely bound anthology featuring my poetry. Another starving artist, I thought to myself. I would just as soon poke needles in my eyes. And I thumbed my nose at these vanities.

My nerves were on edge but I wasn't about to submit myself to this intimidation. Why, this was nothing more than a slap in the face and it only caused me to redouble my efforts. As I recalled the poem that I had sent them I could only remember a few lines. I hadn't kept a copy myself.

"In the sunny fields of the olive branch.

In the wisdom of your booming tide,

Press me one last time and, forever,

Pluck this pestilence from my throat.

Return to me, I beg, my smiling, common clay."

13

Ruminating thus I felt that certainly there lies some recompense in publication, merely a small fee, perhaps, but remuneration nonetheless. All in all what was I being subjected to? So many query letters and so many rejections. The "big book" was coming along but slowly. If I couldn't obtain the comfort of being published by a small piece of my efforts what chance had I of selling a more substantial book. And then, of course, there were the fees for copying and postage which would demand the collection of many bottles and cans. Advertising myself out for work I had made a simple sign. At this I felt a certain amount of shame, the shame that I was no longer a writer and I was selling myself short of my credentials, so to speak. As luck would have it I was to meet a big fellow named John. He was very unassuming and generous and proposed, seeing that I was homeless, that I sleep in his barn and tend to a few chores outdoors and around the house. It was a godsend for it was approaching winter. Soon Christmas would be here and I would be saved from the cold and damp. "Dear Sir," I said to him, "I am a bit weak at the knees, damaged goods from hunger, you might say, but I will make myself worthy no matter what the cost." I wished only to express my gratitude and nothing more or less. He seemed pleased with my docility. He, too, was short on words.

We took his truck and made our way to my stash of few belongings at the river in a pile by the shrubbery. Then we drove out of the rural roads to his little ranch. I was blubbering inside myself with joy. I felt, at once, privileged and safe within his company. At the front house we entered. There he gave to me a more substantial sleeping bag, a down bag, and some toiletries. We sat down to a modest meal for which I was thankful having been without food for a day or two. Yes, he seemed to watch out for me in my frail disposition.

The stable, well, it smelled of manure and piss. However, it wasn't so disagreeable. After all, who was I to complain? I had a roof over my head and a full stomach. My bed was made of straw but it, too, was rather comfortable. Nothing but plusses, I thought to myself.

15

I was to find out that my agenda included waking each day with the animals at about five in the morning. This was the time that Big John would make his entrance. His favorite saying, his motto was "Damned if you do, damned if you don't." Meanwhile, I had befriended the animals such that they had become my dearest friends. Judging from this agreeable and humble setting one would guess that I had no schooling, formal or informal. But it wasn't true. As I wrote in my "big book":

"Long ago when the fashions of youth had disappeared I dove inwardly to seek out covenants left untold, to the Land of Books. And there the litany of words took hold and brought me to my knees and shook my house as in a storm. Among others I then envisioned empires before me crushed by entropy and I scrutinized the text of their wanderings that lay in wait. Still, could I live with this anguish? Oh, but I, I wanted for nothing! Regret to me, it was a useless emotion. For now in the brightening skies the moon is standing quite still and amidst the stars there is but a mad rush."

16

Everyday, I thought to myself, I would feel happier than the last, though I was a blind man eking out each mount. And, of course, I couldn't shake the music from my brain. But up the rungs and down the rungs, I had finally arrived at this modest sanctuary. Here no questions were asked. Outside of humanity I awaited my calling, none the wiser. Among the starts and stops of each unthinking day I was presently surprised at my composure. But the animals knew me, perhaps, better than the people that surrounded me in their neighborhood ranches. Had the animals taken to my timorous self, coaxing them all along? Occasionally I would part from this primrose path asking myself if I could ever replace that which was lost along the way or whether or not I would succeed as a published writer. This, it seemed, was my last bout with pride. And as I have said hunger and the cold were my only sworn enemies.

Today, like all other days, I would rake up the dung while whistling a merry tune. Soon I would venture with Aussie, the Australian shepherd, to herd the animals into the fields. Yes, I was a shep-

17

herd and a happier one nobody ever knew! I would take my staff, as in biblical times, while the sunlight spun its gold. These were my most joyous times. In the evening, somewhere in the sweet song of crickets, lay the window to perpetuity. There is now to my eyes a beginning and an end. Somewhere lay peace, somewhere lay happiness. Why not here? If I had a hapless moment it would one day be gone. In difficult times there was still the wisdom of the body. Such did my walks dictate.

However, after many months, my reflections were sometimes overwhelming. I had reveries to boot. Who could better name my struggles? In the depths of my being, you see, I had been here before. But why does it hurt to speak? Oh, this acumen, there is no telling where it will lead me. Mine is to dismiss it and to shrug. Read the tea leaves and put a happy face on it, you might say. God love ya, but the devil was at my back.

Today the wind could fell a tree. Even with the profoundest pleasure there lies, not too faraway, melancholy and its ken. Vagaries without number, you might propose. But it is turning toward darkness now and the frogs are croaking. Among contentious replies I press on. At the church not faraway I hear the clamor of bells. The winsome vines are gathering the light and the dry grasses are hemming me in amongst the summer's buzz. Not a day passes without my thanks that I am not only alive but exuberant as well.

If there was a hunt for truth this meant surrendering myself to the day, to the animals and the sky above me. But meantime, how was I to sculpt the images of my world? I must discard all that conspired against me. Here I was safe from all human eyes.

To feed the animals had its rewards. As the sun descended there was a lull in activity. Often I would venture outside to witness the advent of dusk. It was my favorite time of day. Oh, twilight when the skies succumb, oh, gentle light, I would moan. It was a perfect liaison with what was rarely an imperfect day.

Daisy, one of the goats, was often tempestuous. Nonetheless, this seemingly offensive trait

19

endeared her to me. In fact, I borrowed strength from her courage to stand up to all beasts. The goatee and horns served only to accent her personality. She would punctuate time banging against her stall.

The pigs would snort and scurry inside their pens as well while Minney, the horse, and her daughter Roslyn would whinny. And, of course, the roosters as was their bent would constantly peck at the ground. Nightfall would usher in the silence and sleep from much toil. Yes, upon the nighttime almost everything would hush but for the summer crickets.

Promptly at dawn the hay and feed would be distributed among the animals. At my morning leisure I would read verses from my favorite poets. Sometimes it only took a few words to fill me with inspiration. I had always been a simple man though I was occasionally guilty of gnawing at the bit, so to speak.

In the morning, as well, I would take a cold shower in the nude behind the stable. After Big John and I fed the animals we would feed ourselves with ham and eggs in the front house. Neither of us spoke much but there was a certain peace understood among us.

Once, in the beginning, we partook of some whisky and smoked cigars. It was at this time that Big John let it out that he had once been in prison. He didn't say much more than this and I didn't want to pry. What more was there to say? Most people have skeletons in their closet. Also, once in a great while, I would accompany him to the market. It was quite a jolt from my solitary self and the animals. However, I took it in stride, astonished by some of the lovely women that frequented such places. Most of them, it appeared, were young mothers.

He had a few acres of vines and he would cordially offer me as much wine as I would want to drink. Such was the bounty of his modest estate, neither too big nor too small.

Aussie and I got along famously, sauntering through the hills and valleys and the ravines of oak. Above us the hawks soared and everyday was a little like the first day of the world. Oftentimes I

21

would wish that I had the exquisite hearing of the animals and parading up and down the slopes I would sing hymns and ditties dedicated to the animals. Such passages and rites each day were profuse. Yes, it was a peasant's life and it pleased me a great deal.

Then one day the ax fell, the unimaginable happened. Big John took deathly ill and it was very soon after that he passed on. And so with the knapsack I had when I first arrived and a tearful farewell to the animals I wandered down the rural esplanade to town bent on finding a new home.

IV

I returned to town with great reluctance. I had, I found, been pampered and spoiled by my rather long sojourn at the stable. I wasn't prepared to tackle financially or otherwise the difficulties that had so suddenly and crudely been thrust upon me. It is true that my writing had suffered from the many hours that my chores had consumed. But it was all that I could do and, once again, I was invigorated to try my hand, believing that there was some talent even if it only lay deeply within. After all it wasn't so much that I had no equal in this regard but that my efforts were beyond reproach. No, I shouldn't apologize for them in any way or manner.

My "big book" had been put on hiatus and it was probably a good idea not to attempt too much in the beginning. No, I must ferret out a smaller bit of turf in which to exercise these rites. Perhaps a short story or a poem about the stable? What matters most is the consummation of my little project and not some massive tour de force. Even though, I must confess, that I possessed a particular hankering for a novel it, I suppose, could wait. For my resources were slender and quite fragile arising, no doubt, from country living as opposed to my city life.

Thinking such thoughts as I walked helped propel me to a small café that I knew had inexpensive cuisine. I had saved a few dollars from the small salary that Big John gave to me from time to time. Entering a little sheepishly I sat down with my pack and took to perusing the menu. It had been such a long while since I was out in public that I found myself retreating from within. I must relax, I thought. I mustn't fall into a state of self-pity which I felt was welling up within. The thrust of my writing endeavors must supersede any and all directions. I must take flight with the words at my disposal making of it an inventive and fruitful past time. After all, there was no dearth of material with which to pummel the public. I would simply have to make substance of the many alleyways that I had traversed. What more of a compelling tale could there be than life in the backyards of so many people.

There was a woman across from me sitting quite upright in her chair. She was counting out the change in her purse oblivious of me. I suddenly felt such a flood of tears coming that I didn't know any longer how to hide. Her solitude seemed to beg for company though I was apprehensive about any such intervention, the likening being much more than I could tolerate. I could see that she was with limited funds and this predica-

24

ment was not only upon my shoulders but hers as well. Yes, I was far too close to simply amusing myself by such circumstances and I chided myself for my cowardice in this direction. One shouldn't grimace at the sight of angels, I muttered to myself, and I proceeded to lunch on my meal as if it was to be my last.

Outside the sky was magnificent, brushstroke for brushstroke, and it made me want to swoon. Had any man been as lucky as I? I wondered. But in contrast the shadows were deepening and my muses were nowhere to be found. The harsh reality of bedtime was upon me. Fortunately I had my good down bag to keep me from the elements and I scurried to the outskirts of town, not too far from a church, to make my stronghold. The sky was now mottled with stars and there was a slight wind that flushed my face. I said goodnight to the animals far away that had befriended me and fell fast asleep from all of the worries and woes of this day, of this world.

The birds awakened me, the birds and the pale light. I still had a modest sum of money for

25

my meals and the postage for my short story in the making. I wasn't used up yet. I hid my meager belongings in the brush as before not wanting to appear the vagrant. But who was I kidding with such postures? Everyone, no doubt, was suspicious of me from the beginning. Meanwhile, words about me were like a fire but I cringed at meeting eye to eye with these brothers and sisters of mine. At the park I rested, sad with my beleaguered opportunities. Startled from my daydreams I mustered the strength to put two words together at a time not wishing to strain any creative impulses. I was hounded by this inferno to make tracks when I wished for nothing more than to make ends meet.

All in all it was a glorious day as I promenaded to the promising riches of my newly sought vocation. Things were going well though I was still shy of completing my tale. Upon this task I merely crept on all fours. I reinstated my post office box intent on making a killing at the publication houses, replies I would undoubtedly receive in this humble and gracious beginning. If such deeds of mine were unwelcome there would, indeed, be absolutely nowhere that I could go.

Down the park esplanade there traipsed a middle aged man and woman. She, by all appearances, looked as though she was wearing a chastity belt, so stiffly did she walk. While he, no doubt, wore a codpiece. At these observations I laughed out loud. Then I took stock, once again, of my own disheveled looks having crumpled clothes from sleeping in them. For a moment, and only a moment, I longed for my past to assert itself. However, nostalgia wasn't my failing and, in fact, though I had little time to cling to such remembrances, my freedoms were many. No, it was the story that was all important and not these momentary inconveniences.

Weeks passed by unremarkably enough. I had used the last of my money to mail my completed story, the story that would resurrect me. My hunger came and went. I had procured a few hours of work per week sweeping and mopping up at a thrift store. My patience had all but disappeared when it arrived. The notice, that is, of my acceptance for publication. I was ecstatic. I waved my hands frantically and I clicked my heels. I finally realized that I had been at my wits' end.

There were a few signatures required and soon a sum of one hundred dollars would be mailed to me. Even the money, though greatly appreciated, was subservient to the shower of accolades such as "an amazing story, expertly told." "An amazing story, expertly told," I repeated over and over. Yes, I wasn't just any old fool, I thought to myself, I was an established and successful author. Henceforth I shall write at breakneck speed. "Until I get it right," was my only rejoinder. "Until I siphon the sumptuous prose that makes a man weep and kittens to purr." My inhibitions must vanish. My writing should open up not emulating a particular result nor crowded into a singular pose. Goodness, man, I was an author with a bright future, I might add.

I pocketed the letter but found myself stopping every few steps to reread its contents. "Amazing, expertly," I blubbered again and again. I was no longer alone in my beliefs of being a writer. No,

28

I was well on my way to a sort of stardom. The first hurdle was, no doubt, the most difficult and if I could manage to publish my "big book" it would be nothing shy of an exceptional performance.

Glowing with the new possibilities of getting off the streets I arrived at a home that was advertising a room for rent. The price was right though the owner seemed to look down upon me. "You're not a troublemaker?" she asked with some authority. I merely beamed with delight showing her the letter of my acceptance. I explained that I was only prepared to pay a fee as a gesture of good faith, so to speak, until the money arrived. She, herself, seemed a little desperate for money and as there were no other prospects to be seen she began to warm to me. In fact she began to name her favorite authors, authors who carried no weight with me. No, I was a master of the word and with my "big book" I would put to shame such impostors and mere has-beens. I told her that I would favor moving in at once. She agreed and I took my knapsack upstairs in a fever to write. However, as if robbed of all intentions, I couldn't so much as dot the paper. Soon I scowled at these encumbrances eventually coming to the conclusion that it would only be a short matter of time before its execution. I was simply too wound up. This seemed to appease my state of urgency for the meanwhile and I soon found myself outdoors taking in the scent of jasmine and pines.

I posted my mail with the signatures requested by the publisher and scurried to a grocery store. Then I fed myself with fruit and nuts feeling all the better for it. Perhaps, I thought, I could have my part-time employment forward me a few dollars until my money arrived. Yes, I would do best to show them all my letter of acceptance without any modesty on my part. Surely they would not only agree but would be pleased to accommodate me. We had, after all, no fuss between us and we rested upon good terms to my knowledge thus far.

As I entered the thrift store I could hear Helen, my boss, singing with an exquisite voice. Oftentimes she would shine, exposing a good mood. It seemed as though the entire world was singing today. In fact I couldn't recall when things looked more rosy than today. My life had swung around so greatly that I, too, felt like singing. I was almost weak at the knees from so much delight. But I paused having doubts and reprimanding myself for assuming a false sense of security. However, why this contrariness, I thought. Was it due to my present writer's block? The blank page never appeared so bleak. "What if I can't pull it off?" I queried. But my racing and expectant mind was getting ahead of me. It was no good ruining this moment of pleasure and gratitude. Instead of applauding my efforts too much I should, perhaps, insult myself a little and have a joyous time of it all.

Helen approached me with good tidings. I presented her with my letter. She became as congratulatory as could be. I broached her with the request that I borrow a few dollars until the arrival of my prize money. Without a qualm she consented and offered me a cup of coffee. The shadows from my diffident self scrutiny began to disappear. Why, if one couldn't on occasion bask in the sun of accomplishment, what sense was there in going on? No, I should do well to rest upon my laurels.

31

She asked me what the story was about and caught me off guard momentarily. Suddenly I became flushed at the prospects of her becoming to know me all too well. Hence, I first balked, and then I invented a story that would be agreeable with her. Neither was I too dark nor too bitter for her study of me. I remained on the middle ground until I had pleased her curiosity. Quickly I went to work on the pretext that I had exhausted, with these few words, the content of my story.

V

On the way home for some reason, I suppose of celebration, I ducked into a bar. I was not accustomed to such places. I took a seat in the back wishing only to dissociate myself from the other patronage. I hadn't had a drink since Big John's stable and memories of the animals came rushing back almost making me sob. The television and stereo music was booming and nobody was talking but for a few hoots and hollers when a team would score. I noticed a couple in a darkened corner espying me in a curious way, making me feel rather uncomfortable. For some solace I brought out a napkin seeking to write my way out of this forlorn condition.

Soon the woman who seemed to take an interest in me arrived at my table. I attempted to be cordial though I felt quite the contrary. I wasn't born yesterday and I had made out her company in the corner as nothing more than a nefarious outlaw and a pimp prepared to roll me at any time. The noise was such that I could barely comprehend her words. However, she began to gesture wildly as though struck by lightening. No doubt she was the recipient of vast quantities of dope and a lush to boot. Meanwhile I stood my ground, so to speak, in complete control of myself as opposed to her shenanigans. It was obvious that she wanted me to support their addictions by whatever foul means. She was inches away from death or religious conversion, I thought to myself.

These same jackasses abound at every bar, I supposed. It was no wonder that I had deliberately avoided them all of these years. She began to nose around in my affairs, inquiring about the napkin and what I was writing and so forth. Well it seemed quite apparent that I didn't have to answer to anyone. Surely she must see that I was, in contrast to her, my own keeper. For lack of direction I began to spin a yarn of truth and fiction. I clutched the acceptance notice in my pocket, remembering who I was, and began to brag about my station in life. Yes, I was a writer and a damned successful one, I crowed to my amusement. I was, in fact, very well off and at this very moment was working on a bit of spadework for my new novel. Hence I was dressed as such.

She smelled of sex and booze. I was reminded of how different my life had been at her age. Once I had loved in such another clime, young and free, when the world was my garden. What she needed was a bucket of lye soap. There wouldn't be any pillow talk with the likes of me, and I smiled, sardonically, at this quip.

As she swayed to and fro I examined the bartender at some distance. This old pappy was fidgeting with himself, as was she, looking as if he had missed the litter box. And I continued on in this same vein telling her of my success in having a book turned into a movie. Yes, soon they would be working in the balconies for me. Vast applause would ring out wherever I roamed. But wait, nothing was so vulgar as her impropriety toward me. She was, it seemed, running out of patience with this flapdoodle, rejecting my claims, and pilfering my mind for a pinch of dope. Suddenly I realized that my conceit was, perhaps, getting me into trou-

35

ble. They were, no doubt, partners in crime and I was no more than a vagrant, my pockets lined with gold. She proceeded to ask my name and then turned the tables by offering me a drink. I saw this ploy from miles off. I graciously declined and she became furious at me for not playing the game. The game, that is, of baiting me with her notebook of courtesy and latter robbing me at will. She asked if I was alone or expecting somebody. At this I paused but upon second thoughts I decided to name a joining party if for nothing more than giving myself an ally.

It didn't sit well with me but I suppose there was no getting around it. My cards had been played and I was merely a victim of my pride and egotism. Yes, I had found myself speaking as though I had been published many times over and that I was every fledgling writer's dream. I continued, for some reason, perhaps to annoy her and her intrusiveness. I sang my praises further and rolled a cigarette, oblivious to her rant. It was time to make tracks and I dismissed myself to the restroom. There I locked the door and climbed through a window making good my escape. The air never felt so sublime. It was evening. Above me there came a hawk's cry and then the utmost silence. I inserted the key and crept upstairs not wishing to speak with anyone. There I took a hot shower and slept the sleep of the dead.

Upon awakening I could hear the owner whistling and humming. I dressed and ran downstairs. There I was confronted with her and she, very generously, offered me some eggs, toast, and coffee. This was a welcome change from last night's soiree with the criminals at the bar. In the future I would have to watch out for these villains not knowing how far they would go to exact a piece of change from me or beat the sense out of me for my aloof manner. I could still recall the face of the pimp at the bar, his eyes hostile and smacking with deceit.

The landlady was most garrulous showing me pictures of her family. Her husband, who was deceased, as well as photos of her son and daughter and their families were happy by all appearances. Yes, another day and everybody was quite happy and though I hadn't written a word since my letter of acceptance I was, nevertheless, filled with optimism. It, after all, had ties with the legitimacy of being published and I crooned to myself the words, "expertly written," and "an amazing story." There was no time to waste. The fire had been lit and it was only a matter of some foreseeable time that I would package my "big book" for my grateful publishers to peruse. Who knows what amenities and remunerations might pass my way?

After receiving my money for the short story I felt like a man of great wealth. But I cautioned myself against spending and kept an eye on a budget of some parsimony. Writing was coming along modestly though I had hoped for a more fruitful outing thus far. The blank paper was making me stall more and more. It was unsettling but not an invincible assault. "Patience," I would counsel myself. To encourage my efforts I would invent pet names designed to lift my spirits and make light of my enterprises. In my opinion I was simply too stiff with formality. I must loosen my wings to fly.

38

I must bust out of these shackles, I would declare. Then I would slump into a stupor unable to put two words together. Time to pound away, I would curse. No need for inhibitions or any such buckram. Sometimes it would work and at other times, without rhyme or reason, I would fail miserably.

I walked down the main thoroughfare rehearsing the drama of my "big book" when I came upon a guitar player on a bench. Seemingly he was homeless. He reminded me of my old self and I coughed up a few coins to put into his opened guitar case. I sat down upon the lawn and mused about my creation. Suddenly I was filled with a revelation. Perhaps I should write another short story as a quick fix for my financial well being. With another short story the end to my novel would be in sight. I was inspired by this plot, the money I might profit, and the freedom to pursue my "big book" as I saw fit. I couldn't think of a dark side to this insight. Anyway, I was slowly becoming displaced by this truncated form of endeavor though it suited me well. It was beginning to dawn on me that I was no longer a vibrant youth. I was middle-aged and, before I knew it, I would soon be in my senior years. I needed to latch onto something that would distinguish me above all others. But surely there were other late bloomers.

Each day I would scurry to the post office expectant of a new acceptance into my little hall of fame. But each day for a month now I would be sorely disappointed. Perhaps my original publication was no more than a fluke, I would question. However I had doctored up my present submission over and over until it held water, so to speak, and it appeared to me to be superior to my first story. Surely there would be a reprieve from this indifference. Surely there would be more accolades. My acceptance letter had now been crushed as I repeatedly referred to its content, an expression of reward and honor that I wouldn't soon forget.

But for now it was a summer's day in winter and I was lapping up the sunlight. The fellow with the guitar had disappeared. I wondered, as before, why I had the dubious distinction of fanning all other parties away from me. Was it merely a nudge of fortuity or was there some truth to the basis of these retreats? Was there recourse to all of these affronts to my soul? Rejected by people and publishers alike was I a mere has-been unfit for a society in which to dwell comfortably? In this connection I was reminded with grave lament of Big John and his ranch. Who knows, if I was eventually successful with my "big book" I might very well find myself in similar lodgings. In this turnabout of thought I concluded optimistically that the sky was the limit. Fortunately, for the time being, I had not quit my employment at the thrift store. It pleased me a great deal to work hand in hand with Helen.

Sometimes I would shelve used books. This was my favorite past time and I would often peruse their content hoping one day to see my name on the jacket of my "big book." These days Helen's voice was even more mellifluous than before and I had, in fact, procured a small but flattering raise in my wages. Meanwhile, Christmas was on the horizon and I made a point of it to purchase candles for my landlady and Helen as well. At this time last

41

year I was comfortably installed in my little stable. This Christmas I was determined to dig in and join society as never before. You might say that I was incorrigible but, in truth, I am only modestly stubborn and greatly patient when you consider some of the trespasses I have suffered. Hitherto and straightaway I must impale these phantasms at my side with good sense, using a shield and sword of my words to corral them into their pens.

Tonight when the stars glisten from faraway and the moon is everywhere to be found I place a homemade wreath on a monument at the center of town. It is a tribute to a man who had been called The Greeter in our little township. I do not know why I felt so obliged but there was an affinity to this man of which I was certain. I would be interested in company such as his though I couldn't very well find good conscience involving others in my inexplicable drama. But the curtain has been raised to my writing and I find nothing more than a script of a poor tragedienne. I am entirely without magnetism and all my nuptials had come to pass. I was as lonely as this Greeter without his acceptance.

In the midst of this night at his statue I am humbled by his presence and I derive great strength from the character that he portrayed. He was a loner and a man like me eking out a livelihood as best he could. How many times had he gone hungry and without shelter like myself? His glory is my glory! But I am sitting well for now and I am not without my resources. I shall not pass the chalice before my time is through. I have nothing left to sacrifice but the vague murmurings of my heart and soul. Huddled by this tombstone of sorts I turn to see a moon rising and it alights upon my shoulders and the facsimile of this man that has come to pass. Meanwhile, this has come to me as if an omen. I stand dusting myself off and I saunter away whistling a merry tune.

The images are now coming in great drifts and I am confounded by their sheer numbers. I cannot wait to write! I await their calling on bended knees. I sit myself down upon the stoop of the store next door to the thrift shop. With my racing mind I feel that I might go raving mad. Punctuated

43

for a brief respite at times I revel at the summit of these creations finding no fault with their caprice. In other words their lame excuses, their bullying, and their probing in all of the inventions of the mind. But the words are presently passing through me like a sieve and I grow incapable of capturing them no matter the speed that I write. It is bothersome but there still exists a fund of words and memory that only a man half-possessed can deliver. Despite the agitation I must triumph. I must learn the tricks of composure. I must find my peculiarities and exploit them. I must insist on their agenda but conforming to my own. I shall not lose confidence. I will hail down these words as the greeter hailed down traffic by his poses and peering at some distance I will let the spectacle unfold. But please ease my mind soon, I tell myself, for I am contorting into grunts and groans, agonies and anguish, without the least deliberations or presumption.

At home I sit in my overstuffed chair, feet on the ottoman, suffering these last throes of the imagination and recuperating from the several blows and vast interruptions of this outburst. My hands are now idle and my mind is without substance. I am, once again, singularly possessed. I have labored to the point of madness and I lay exhausted. My visitants, my muses, have run sweetly by without discrimination and my replies have been swift and final. Such reflections would no longer wither on the vine. Feeling consumed I bite my lip and lay my head upon the pillow, and doze and doze.

VI

I began talking to myself more and more just as before I met Big John. With my continual thirst I felt like I might very well be on the verge of diabetes. However, I couldn't afford seeing a doctor and, too, it was only a small nuisance as long as I kept a bottle of water near.

At my desk upstairs you could find me more than not pouring over notes for a short story as well as working on my "big book." Occasionally my landlady, Nanny, would make cookies and cakes for me.

45

If I discovered a new idea, paragraph, or a sentence I would pounce upon it with diabolical glee. That, or, I would stare dumbly at my acceptance letter with faraway dreams. At still other times I would gaze preternaturally at the rafters in my room, hovering above the notes that seemed insulting. Then abruptly I would pummel the page with a persistent fever of writing that was my cornerstone, you might say. But too often loathsome of these same notes I would fill the trash can and spit at my efforts with utter derision.

By afternoon, if I was not working at the thrift shop and if it was Saturday, I would walk with great and determined haste to the book fair. It was here at the park where I was prepared for introductions into the world of publishers. Well, it was new to me but I wasn't going to let myself hang in the wind. No, I wouldn't allow them to take me for granted as a middle-aged upstart unworthy of their attention. The thrust of the matter was that I present myself as a published author capable of a prize and money and insistent upon their serious considerations. I wouldn't be turned away without due regard. I must be considered seriously, as I say, and I shouldn't be moved until I am distinguished from the anonymous crowd. Easier said than done, for I would too often turn from them in terror of their stupid looks, jabbering to myself and leaving no profanity spared. What a travesty and deception, I would declare. They must answer me plainly! Was I entirely without talent and should I be digging ditches at some lonesome gravesite? Chasing after their own tails, let them, I would rally. According to 'them' and the negative response to my many query letters the public wasn't ready for such dramatics that lean toward tragedy. Write a 'how to' book one of them once said to me. Imagine that, these diagnosticians telling me from their perch "how the cow ate the cabbage."

Though the fall has come and gone and it is in the midst of the holidays I am still adamant about being published. However, I am no longer without reservations. The barren interlude between the present and my one and only acceptance has, indeed, been sobering. But now I was comparatively wealthy with the luxury of a room and board and some agreeable employment. The thing of it is to not take yourself too seriously. When the time was ripe things would swing full circle. Nonetheless, often I would tell myself that I was simply spent and take a holiday from the pen.

Such was the case when I met Elaine, a dear friend of Helen. There was nothing about the day that would portend of this meeting. The clouds were lowering and the sky was washed out. Meanwhile I was busy dissecting some abstract notion of time and place when I discovered her at the stoop of the thrift shop. Our eyes seemed to meet one another at the same time. Her dog barked happily as if expecting a treat. Deep inside my voices seemed to scamper away and I was filled with a sense of well being. My heart was turning away from negation and toward love's embrace. I could feel myself crying out in desperation. When I spoke to her my emptiness was gone and I felt as though the hoax of this life of mine had vanished. Though it was quite sudden I felt like getting down on my knees and asking her forgiveness as though I had betrayed her. Don't you see? It was the culmination of all of these awkward and difficult times to rediscover myself in the mirror of her generous face. It was only natural to take solace in the gift of this moment and I did so without recriminations of any kind.

I was flushed with fever for her but I must bring to bear the patience of conversation, I thought, not hurrying anything along as these numberless ideals ran through my mind. All of my lonely haunts seemed like so much dust to me now. My fables thus far were only so much fodder and felicity arose from my trials with free reign. I felt that my beard and hair must be shorn to lose the hideous mask I had worn for some time now. But too many thoughts and images were flitting by without surcease. Self-consciousness was burrowing in and was being driven into me like nails. Was it one and the same with her? Still I was, as anybody might well be, tired of running amok through the streets day and night. Perhaps this was my finest hour!

I excused myself telling her that I would be a little late to work and I walked intently to the barber shop. The barber seemed to scowl at my appearance and the duration of time it would take to cut my hair and shave my beard. Not a word was said during the half hour it took to perform the task. Nevertheless I tipped him generously feeling like a newborn. Then I made haste to the store to buy some Christmas candles for my two gals and Nanny.

Arriving at work I was completely unrecognizable. Announcing myself the girls looked in awe and told me that I had lost twenty years. I said as much myself and I presented my gifts to them. Feeling a little timorous with my new bald face and shorn hair I succumbed to their gratitude and began shelving a pile of used books. Later in the day we washed Elaine's dog, Peanuts. She and Helen were now both living upstairs above the thrift shop and they brought me there to partake of some dessert. Having traveled from back east Elaine's belongings and creature comforts lay strewn over the living room floor. It was my first visit there and I was quick to detect Helen and the likeness to herself.

50

Startled by my appearance my landlady voiced similar observations toward my new look as had Helen and Elaine. Then she took me to the living room to meet her family. They had just arrived from far to the north and were kicking back from the fatigue of their journey.

The following day at work I was confronted by Helen. Elaine had gone shopping and she mentioned, off the cuff, that she was sweet on me. She asked playfully if we had met before. I replied, no, with a simper and I shyly turned away. When Elaine arrived I was reminded of her affections. We giggled like children or as if we were lovers that had first lain with one another. We spent the rest of the day window shopping and once, while quietly walking, Elaine took me by the arm.

Back at home there was a knock at the door. It was Christmas Eve and Nanny extended an invitation to me to share dinner. As I wasn't dining at Helen's until tomorrow I gratefully accepted. It would seem that I was no longer merely a lonely boarder inhabiting an attic space, no, appeals and covenants seemed to congregate about me as never before.

Sitting around the dinner table I felt as though I was responsible for the heavy silence and as though I should account for my time. To this end I began to trot about with some conceit over my publication and the incisive stories that lay in wait. The gist of my efforts, it would seem, was my "big book" but this would take some time with revisions and so forth. But the conversation seemed to drift away from the focus of my chit-chat and I felt like I had lost an appreciative audience. They seemed to look upon me as a nuisance that had infringed upon their mother's good will. And so, before dessert, I dismissed myself graciously and as if a man of some distinction I strolled upstairs to my room. I stared at the parcel of my latest manuscript on the bed. It was a tale loosely based upon Big John and the animals. It was, but for the postage, ready to be sent to another one of these indifferent publishing houses.

The next day, bright and early, I arrived at Helen's. From there we traipsed downstairs for my presents. Not being well off themselves they still offered me whatever clothes I wanted. I told them I hadn't a clue as to what I should pick. And so anxiously they started to make me over from head to foot. They proceeded to pull out a handsome sports jacket, a sweater and two shirts, two pairs of pants, a pen and paper, and a beret that made me look as though I was from the Left Bank. My writer's hat, they affectionately called it. I had never been showered with so many gifts my entire life and I almost began to sob. Sensing my emotion they both hugged me and led me upstairs with my new duds for a bite to eat. After dinner I proposed that we take a walk to the park. Helen declined, no doubt to encourage our tryst. Romantic or not, at the least, we had commenced upon a friendship that would insure joy.

Oh, but her radiance was without equal! It was enough to overwhelm me ten times over. She wasn't just another treacherous feline. She was down to earth in every syllable that she uttered. Although she was very interested in my writings I couldn't be forced to acquiesce to them. They, after

53

all, paled in comparison to real life and since meeting her my words only served to oppress me. I was becoming a new man at the threshold of love and I wanted to press myself against her and sacrifice the train of these words that once owned me. Yes, once upon a time they had meant everything to me and now they merely lay in the shadows, forsaken in the darkness. I would gladly give them up for a sonnet of love about Elaine. Anything, that is, that came close to my feelings for her. I found myself pleading for some reconciliation, something honorable and without hesitation but it wasn't forthcoming. What justice could be done to match with exuberance an adequate portraiture of her? No, I was stymied.

It seemed absurd that I couldn't resume my story telling in face of this dilemma but it was true and with it came the realization that I wouldn't be able to finish my "big book" with these ambiguities in question. From a distance everything seemed conceivable, nonetheless, upon closer scrutiny the execution wasn't plausible. Perhaps it was only my naiveté to consider both things at once, for I wanted both things to be true and comprehensible despite the contrary.

At home I was cornered by Nanny. She had obviously taken up with the champagne and surprised me by asking if I was in love and what was happening to me with my new looks and my new clothes. I shied away not wanting her to discover my life and changes but I said, very simply, that it was possible. At one time I had thought that she had been in my room. I had no lock. Was she nosing around in my papers and my affairs? But in the end I couldn't be sure and nothing was ever said about it.

I showered and tried on my clothes like a new groom. Excited by my new appearance I began to whistle "Here Comes the Bride" and I broke down laughing, calling myself a writer and a dandy. My vanity didn't end here. I sat down and wrote an ode to Elaine. Nothing that I wished her to see, mind you, but something strenuous that appeased these strong feelings within. I retrieved my "big book" and soon began laughing again. All of my genuine efforts seemed smashed against my current streak of giddiness and I told myself to trash it rather than continue with its execrable creation.

In the morning, in the same giddy mood, I donned my new sports coat, sweater, and pants. I snatched my beret and manuscript and I swaggered outdoors to meet the day. First I delivered my short story to the post office and then I had coffee out swearing off any more writing. Let my expertise rankle the public, I thought to myself. My heart and soul were too intact to write any longer so complacent was I.

Next I visited with Helen and Elaine who were beginning their day inventorying some merchandise that had been dropped off the night before. Elaine sidled by me making me catch my breath, and teased me with a fit of laughter. I sometimes felt as though I was a child, she was so much more seasoned at love affairs. Sophisticated, you might say. But in the birth of these feelings I was already wondering when the ardor would disappear. Always ahead of myself, spoiling the moment and entertaining the bitter ties of a questionable future, that was my awkward disposition. "Easy does it," I counseled myself several times.

She clasped my hand and led me upstairs. Giggling like school children, our faces flushed, we emerged from the bed. Completeness was finally mine. Passion had held us in its arms as we awoken from the charms of love. Washing away all the many cares and the din of bad memories happiness was now ours and it wouldn't easily be forgotten. This much was certain. It was enough to make you sing each others praises, and to move gingerly within the dream. My eccentricities loomed everywhere but they only served to put a smile on Elaine's face whenever they arose.

VII

I say these things coming from afar, for a tragedy has struck. It is not the ultimate tragedy of a loss of life but a loss, nevertheless, of livelihood and possessions. A fire has displaced Helen and Elaine. As I approached the gutted building I espied them both with the dog. Apparently he had barked in the middle of the night awakening them amidst the smoke. Fortunately they were able to make it out though they had lost everything in the struggle. They would have to relocate back East where they had family. Their loss was mine as well. For I, too, would not only be out of work but without friends as well. I was reminded that the pendulum swings both ways. Having experienced these feasts of life for a short spell I was presented with the dark side once again and once again these voices of the netherworld began to howl at me. Everything appeared bleak so that when I saw them both off at the train station I was blubbering and losing control of my feelings. Suddenly I was pitifully alone and without recourse to writing. At the same time I could feel myself ratcheting up my defenses for survival. "One thing at a time," I wailed to myself.

One month passed by without any kind of work. I was too frightfully alone to take out my "big book." I expressed my dilemma to the landlady. Though sympathetic she, nevertheless, couldn't keep me here for free, she said. I told her that I understood and to make her burden lighter I packed up what belongings I could manage. I took out my sleeping bag and a heavy jacket. All of a sudden haunting memories began to surface from this memorabilia and I couldn't wait to dash out of sight.

The clouds like great swathes marked the sky and there was a bitter chill to the air. Rain was on the way and I felt barely alive. Promises of reuniting with Helen and Elaine seized my mind and flooded my soul. But presently all seemed lost. I felt as though I was falling and my stomach ached for want of food. Where did providence lie? First the fire and then eviction.

I checked my mail at the post office but there was still no reply from the publishing houses. However, and more importantly, there were a few postcards from the girls. I turned on my heels and made tracks to the stream. I wanted to read them over and over but I baited myself to prolong the pleasure. After all, in their presence, I was a man and not a mere boarder or a misfit. In the name of love I wasn't even an author for that matter. I was loved for who I was, plain and simple.

I took out a tarp from my bag and sat beneath a tree in the rain. I read very slowly and deliberately, lapping up each word, savoring the faces that came to mind. Would they, with a little time, forget me as had my publishers?

The rain wouldn't let up and I fancied the warmth of the library. I found myself stowing away my gear so as not to look like a bum and headed in that direction. I pulled out a free newspaper from the vending machine to use as an umbrella and hastened to my destination. It was quiet but you could still hear the rain pelting down from the edges of the roof and upon the enormous windows. The reversion to my past was quick, severe, and complete. I picked out a book that had, once upon a time, been not only one of my favorites but a mentor as well. Sadly disappointed I lay my head down from the exhaustion of the day's activities and fell into sleep. I had lurid dreams of drowning while others looked upon me with profound indifference and I awoke with a start. Judging by the clock I had only been asleep for some fifteen minutes.

I was reminded, for some reason, of my former obsession of counting objects to the denomination of fifteen and I began, momentarily, to resume this practice. I chewed on an old stick of gum I had found in my pocket to cut my appetite and lumbered outdoors. My goal was to retrieve bottles and cans for recycling so that I might purchase a bite of food. I decided that, this accomplished, I would make the move from the woods to a church nearby. No, I wasn't used up yet, I thought to myself, and I thumbed my nose at these devils that seemed to surround me. I wasn't sure if this was merely false bravado but it served to raise my spirits for the time being.

I wasn't the only one at the church. Others congregated under its eaves jabbering away and making obscene gestures, no doubt, to bolster their self confidence. One of them, presumably the leader, was more boisterous than the others. They had lit one of the iron drums ablaze and were gathering in its warmth. They seemed to look upon me with some discrimination, incredulous with smiles, and skeptical of my agenda. Soon they flagged me over, thrusting forth a bottle of liquor. So as not to become ejected from the premises I assented, treading lightly in word and manner, and offering them a stick of beef jerky. Soon their curiosity began to wane and nighttime was well upon us. Having swilled their drink everyone went their own way, but stayed reasonably close to the ash cans for warmth. Whatever might come to pass I was more comfortable here amidst company and a fire than in the woods. And I thought to myself, momentarily, that at least they would be in my 'big book.' Besides what did any of them know being so obtuse in manner and speech. I answered to no man here nor would I ever!

The next day I received my rejection notice from the publisher I had queried. There and then it was settled. I would write with such ardor that nobody could refuse. I would make an itinerary that would eclipse all previous efforts. My tour de force was in the making. I could feel it emerge like parturition. At the library I would write until fatigue set in. I would take a nap and then continue. It is said that "adversity introduces a man to himself." If these words are true one can respect my disposition. My entire life was now consumed by this book. Even in my insomnia, especially in my insomnia, I only wrote that much more. I felt as though I was being swallowed up. Nevertheless, with each exposure, each fragment, I discovered that I was bandaging my wounds. It was clear to me now that the title of the "big book" would be *Tyranny and the Devil* and about this I was adamant. Having such a title gave to me the prerogative of implementing a needle and thread to my imaginings. A thread that would have the elasticity to weather the most brutal of storms and the most untamed writing. At least I held this in good faith.

The light upon my shoulders coursed through my vessels and pounded in the pulse of my neck. With this throbbing came new and fresh impulses that freed me up to write. Enormous drifts of words would alight upon me such as I had never before known. I nearly bleated out "Enough!" at this firestorm but there was no way around it. I felt faint and I couldn't write fast enough. The slightest encroachments to my senses would be manifested in vast Sophoclean themes. They would come about as though hunting me down without cessation and they made it clear that I was their victim and not the other way around. Just as I thought that they were diminishing they would flourish with a set of new intentions, deracinating me with great ease and making me gasp with each provocation. In a stupor I would close my eyes only to be flooded by new appeals and entreaties, adjuncts, and *disjecta membra* from previous chapters.

No doubt others looked upon me as if I was a freak, an eccentric with the manners of a goat and three sheets to the wind. Meanwhile, back at the church, I would be introduced to the homeless recruits in town. Too cold to sleep I would join these dubious others in a stiff drink. Without the luxury of light I would be forced to ignore anymore intrusions from these word mongers, swearing them off one by one. Sometimes I would have to stifle a scream so severe were their provocations.

On this particular night it was so very cold that I had to imbibe heavily an abundance of alcohol that was being served up. I put on all the clothes that I had to help warm me and chattered my teeth at the fire where there was no dearth of tall tales being told. Here there was no accountability and the lies flourished. I tried to collect my thoughts but the liquor had assaulted my mind such that there was nothing to be done about it. At least I felt, for the time being, that there was a comfortable respite to these voices and their demonizing and I welcomed the inebriation with opened arms. Resting my eyes I recalled the faces of Helen and Elaine and I called upon my blessings with gratitude. Only if this maddening inwardness would cease or at least subdue itself. But upon awakening thee was no such luck. One word would again be followed by another and they all begged not only for attention but to be committed to paper as well.

I was the first one awake. I stashed my gear and took my knapsack with my notebook of writings, the paper and pen from my beloved, and hurried to the library. Between then and now I had to stop along the way to accommodate and record these epistles of the night, as I liked to call them. But was I becoming nothing more than a host to madness? My lack of wits was disarming me. To break the mania I decided to collect bottles and cans. On my route I passed by the town memorial of The Greeter. Here I stopped for a few vocal words to his honor and glory. But not wishing to become an ass to the public I crept away after only these brief accolades and resumed my quest for money in the gathering of recyclables.

I stopped by a drug store and bought a post-card for the girls. In it I merely said "Steeped in my big book. Things are going well. I miss you and long to see you again!" I averred with these words not wishing to reveal my crisis as it stood. In short, I was the prevaricator of good news.

Soon it was getting dark and I pedaled my way back home to the ash can and fire. All in all it was a productive day though I had truncated my time with the "big book." I took notice that one of the windows of the church had been broken. Probably to provide shelter from the cold. I began to wonder if this would only get us all into trouble with the law. However, the night only passed with little resistance and deviation from the norm. I was happy the next day to return to my book.

At the library, contrary to recent times, I struggled with writing. The tap had been turned off. It was painful to meet this obstruction and I clenched my fists at this grave interlude. No longer possessed by my muses I began to mourn the death of these words and the elevation of spirit that once was mine. I sat there watching the branches lean with the onslaught of rain. In pursuit of these piteous words I lacked the virtue to resume and soon packed my gear to return to the church.

Upon approaching the premises I noticed that the police had arrived. Since it was paramount that I retrieve my belongings, namely my sleeping bag, I ventured forth. I soon found out that we were all to be brought in for vandalism and vagrancy among other things and that my possessions would be brought to the county jail. First we were padded down, then handcuffed like common criminals. It didn't seem so bad what with the promise of warmth and food but I found myself a little deject-ed behind the bars.

VIII

We were supplied with orange overalls, like flight suits, and then we were led in different direc-tions. I broached my cell with a jailor that seemed to be tongue-tied and defeated. I heard the cell door close with finality. The television mounted on the ceiling was blaring and its deafening roar was cutting into me as had the noise at the bar months earlier. At the top of the far wall I could make out a small window and the distant sky, a patch of blue. I winced from this painful separation from the outdoors and curled up in my bunk. I began to feel as if the city had been sacked and I wondered where lay the victors.

Next to me a man was crying out "I'm no snitch" repeatedly and together with the television was vying for my attention. Occasionally he would try to splash water on me with a cup. Night fell but there was no surcease from this demon nor was there any respite from the noise of the television.

The next morning breakfast was served and I devoured it having not eaten the day before. I was soon feeling better and I lay back dreaming of my beloved. However, momentarily, there arrived the jailor who took me downstairs to an empty room. Shortly a man and woman arrived. They introduced themselves but my mind seemed to be elsewhere. In this state of absentia I believe that the gentleman referred to himself as a doctor. Nevertheless, I couldn't be sure. They seemed to be sympathetic, no doubt, due to my integrity and forbearance. They began to ask me questions to which I hemmed and hawed trying to reply equivocally. Judging from the nature of their interrogations they had perused my "big book." They seemed to be suspicious of me and my state of mind. The eccentricities of my book were coming into question and I wasn't sure how to escape the directness of their considerations. Therefore I merely looked down at the ground with a certain numbness as they stared at me with grandiose curiosity. I felt as though I had been here forever when it finally appeared that I would be dismissed. They had concluded that I was in need of some medicine and explained very succinctly that I would feel better once I had consumed it. I didn't object in the least, seeing no point in it, though I wasn't sure that I needed it. My only closing remark was to request a pen and paper to which they gladly assented. I ingested the medicine and was soon on my way.

Back at my cell I was accosted by this relentless noise. I sat there jabbering to myself about their questions which were only now coming into focus. Perhaps they had mistaken me for a particular character in my book or, worse yet, they had been forced to do it by spurious means. But for now, delighted with my pen and paper, I scribbled a few notes surprised at my clarity with the vast interruptions of noise. Without sunlight the day passed by anonymously. What with the television and this jackal next to me I felt like shouting aloud.

Suddenly I succumbed to fatigue due, without question, to the medicine and its heavy sedation. I was awoken when my food arrived but I had a difficult time disengaging myself from sleep. I quickly consumed my meal and lay back in the uncertain arms of my fate. I slept the entire night through awakening only once to urinate.

When morning came I felt that I had lost any remnants of a racing mind and there was, even for me, a more gentle disposition. I tried to write but I was too exhausted to do so much as scribble a few belabored thoughts. My only solace came now from the drugs and no longer from my writing as before. I felt as though I had lost a dear friend but there was no way around it and my lack of ambition soon no longer disappointed me. Yes, rather than humor, I quietly smiled and my peevish disposition toward my neighbor subsided as well. Inside this capsule of my brain was fluttering with calm and well being and I couldn't protest in the least. The irony of my situation is that I had put a pretty face on it all. A state of mild bliss was now my station. The candle was no longer burning at both ends and I was merely the instrument of their will. In other words, the fight, flight, and fuck had been yanked from me without protest of any kind.

71

If I wasn't sedated I would invariably try to bring them, my caregivers, to see reason. However without any abusiveness these halcyon days were only to be absorbed and resolved quietly. This song and dance was being played out and they weren't about to find any objections on my part. As far as I could see 'they' didn't have any scruples about prescribing such a drug and I only mildly disputed their authority. I was rapt in the hushed glory of this medicine feeling a little like a bimbo. Writing a book now only seemed like nothing more than vanity and foolishness and my mind could only dabble within the confines of this drug. But there was a feeling that I had been vanquished, sacrificed in some respect, though I didn't know how to remedy it. My wounded groin made me feel a little like a nance and my sexual fire was missing. Nevertheless my soul was intact despite these misgivings, and though I was rendered somewhat speechless, my mind was coherent as well.

At the next meeting with my caregivers I blurted out "I am not without a soul, don't you know," and then I wondered why I had said this.

They asked me what I meant and I could only add "What are your intentions?" Toward which I resigned myself half-possessed by this medication. "No," they replied. "You are not without a soul and our intentions are to make you healthy once again." I searched for an argument but none came and I resigned myself to their concerns in an instant. They asked me if I had voices or great fears. "Sometimes," I equivocally answered. "How about now?" they continued. And I told them honestly, no. They seemed very pleased at this reply and told me that I was being treated for schizophrenia. I baulked at this wondering what had made them arrive at such a conclusion. They merely said that oftentimes the homeless were mentally disabled and what was more they had gleaned some pertinent facts from my book *Tyranny and the Devil*. They insisted that they only had the intentions of good will and that they wanted to see me with shelter, food, and peace of mind. In this connection they had sought after a board and care facility to take me under its wings. However, the ultimate response was mine and mine alone. Not wishing to

73

return to the river or the church I immediately consented a little relieved at this conclusion.

Besides my ambitions had deteriorated and there was no hope of procuring both food and shelter with my state of mind. I asked them if I might see my book but they were against this for reasons untold. They met without resistance and I was dismissed until tomorrow when the social worker would arrive to see me. As I was weary of the many perils in my life I began to consider my new lodging with gratitude. Why, it wouldn't be so bad, I thought, to receive food and shelter instead of this homeless squalor. At least for now I was remorseless at such a resolution. I could easily depart if it didn't agree with me, I summarized.

At my bunk I closed my eyes and mused happily about the orchards of my youth. No longer blessed or accursed by these fertile images I found myself nearly dreamless. But for the dreamy appearance and disappearance of a black ocean as if covered by a pall or shroud I was cast out to sea with only a murmur of discontent. A mere glaze, throbbing at the fringes, I took unto my bosom the

74

poverty of my mind. My invisibility was manifest and in low tones came the suspiration of passing voices. A part of me wished only to fling myself from this perimeter while the greater part of me longed for survival. Oh, gentle boy, gentle I rehearsed to this great suppression.

Meanwhile, had anybody missed me, I wondered, or had I come and gone unnoticed? Where had the others from the church gone? Had they returned to a similar haunt? Had I been placed alone with others that were disabled? I longed to be away from this asylum and I couldn't wait to visit with my social worker and quietly disappear. But my exhaustion took hold soon in a form that was forgiving and I surrendered again to a deep sleep.

My worker arrived bringing numberless questions to ask me. It seemed that I was to be transported to a house known as a safe haven for a brief stay of two weeks before being assigned to a permanent facility. There more paper work would be in order so that I might procure the funds with which to live. Until then it would be up to county monies. In a sense I felt as though I was swindling the public. But with this profound numbness all that I was able to do was to lisp or to smile. The height and depth of my yearning had come to pass and I felt estranged from these proceedings. I would count the hours before I was to arrive at this safe haven. There I would luxuriate in the vast, blue sky and with other patrons as need be.

Following our meeting a deep and fundamental silence visited me and it merely said sleep, sleep. On no uncertain terms I was to leave today for this halfway house. Any happiness was quieted by this medication. However, it still reigned deep inside the abyss where lived my soul. The jailor awakened me from my slumber and I was, once again, led downstairs to don my civilian clothes. I sat down with my belongings with a faraway look and peered incisively at my book, *Tyranny and the Devil*. Far more than just comprehensible I approached it with renewed vigor. My counselor walked by eying me with deep curiosity but I was too steeped in my book to pay much attention. The shadow play and the suffering stood out in the re-

76

cesses of the book detectable to the least discerning eye. The form it assumed was both hideous and sublime and I thought, without reservations, that antiquity would be proud. Yes, my will had asserted itself with newborn profundity and in its wake there lay the arousal of instinct and impulse that was rare these days. I began to think of my past life leaving no stone unturned. Oh, my muses, I murmured, embracing my book with a prolonged sigh.

Walking down the hallway, streams of light were more and more evident as we became closer to the exit. Upon opening the door a flood of sunlight assailed my vision and I winced at this with great joy. I hadn't been in a car for ages and it appeared that people were driving in a colossal rush. A part of me wondered, as other times before, if they were congregating on my behalf. With the traffic there came a shoal of timid whisperings but there was a stillness that made me a little misty. There was no longer any surrender to my caprice and I became visibly excited at my new prospects. Finally I had made my departure and I was at my temporary home of the crisis center, removed from jail and its darkness.

IX

One week had passed and I was pleased with my new surroundings; the employees, and the patients. For the most part everybody was quite subdued. To be sure there were no more screams as in jail and the sunlight inundated me with good cheer. Despite the impedimenta of the drugs I was able to, occasionally, work on my book. I found that with each entry I was growing more astute. The others didn't appear to be sick and I sometimes felt that this was nothing more than a hoax. The only unusual circumstance was a fellow who painted his toenails and fingernails. Meanwhile my time was punctuated with the chores of vacuuming, dishwashing, and so forth and I would often wash the employee's cars for a pack of cigarettes. When this wasn't available I would gather cigarette ends from the grounds and at other times

I would join in on a game of volleyball or help plant a garden.

During the second week we all took a trip to the thrift store. This reminded me dearly of Helen and Elaine, and I felt my eyes tear up. How far had I come through all of these trials alone. Would the girls recognize me or would they turn from me not knowing any longer who I was. Often we would hold classes on the nature of our illness or sit on the porch gabbing about this and that. My social worker was Australian and she had a manner to her that was absolutely endearing. All in all they treated me with the utmost respect. Perhaps this was due to my conceit of writing a book and having a short story published. As before I was now tired of my beard and long hair and I managed to borrow a razor and a pair of scissors.

Each day seemed to pass by with more clarity though I frequently napped. I began to grow a little anxious at my prospective home wondering if it was akin to this safe haven or was nothing more than a house of cards. In fact I asked them if I might stay on but they were adamant about the

79

rules and assured me that if it wasn't for policy they would surely accept me. And so after breakfast, at one of the meetings, I bade farewell. I hoisted my knapsack with my book upon my shoulders and scuttled outside to my ride to the board and care.

Well, I didn't feel the earth move but it was certainly a welcomed start. I was liberal with my manners and the management and I had become illustrious in our terms. There were four men and two women. I shared the room with a fellow that kept on chattering but with my medicine I was able to all but ignore it.

Finally, upon retrieving my mail from the post office, I gave my forwarding address. Meanwhile there were two letters from the gals. They appeared worried and what was more invited me to stay with them. This met with my overwhelming approval. Although it wasn't plausible with my limited funds I was well on my way to earning some money from gardening and at night I found myself watching over a group of young boys at a boarding house. There I had plenty of time to work on my book. For transportation I had repaired an old motor scooter and I often took rides through the countryside.

Everybody else went off in the morning to social programs leaving me alone until three o'clock. When they returned the two dogs would start up barking. Together we would sit smoking one cigarette after another not saying much but occasional gibberish. Often, after gardening in the morning hours, I would venture out to a coffee house with one of the managers, William. There I would find conversation and dialogue rather than the strange piecemeal of discourse with the other tenants. Sometimes I was stirred with emotion with William's accommodating remarks. He treated me as if I wasn't debilitated and I was touched even in my sedation. Gardening, too, was most pleasing and I discovered myself whistling while I worked at bagging the copious leaves of autumn. Though I didn't wish to be callous there were more times than not when I avoided the other patients. My thoughts were that I would do best staying close to the employees. There was, after all, nothing to speak of in their presence and the silence surrounding them was deafening.

There was a man named Charles who had attended a private school back East and only became ill while visiting his father, an engineer in Saudi Arabia. While he was by far the worse off he possessed a sense of humor that was quite delightful. The closest to his disposition was that of a fellow who never showered. He would awake leaving before management had rose to avoid this simple task and his bed sheets, I noticed, were stained bright yellow. Upon reflection I believe that I had once seen him parading around town with a brown paper bag over his head. Arriving home he would sit down and chain smoke until dinner. Becoming more and more loquacious he would speak with great enthusiasm toward his revered baseball team. With untamed zeal he would launch into their line-up and their batting averages savoring every word. He was so keen with his observations that one would wonder at his illness. Another fellow would drag about carrying his tape player and playing the same songs day and night. He had the worst frame of mind and would continually frown. I discovered that he had stayed for years at a lock down facility and one could easily espy his spiteful self. He was usually speechless and held such contempt that it was insulting just to sit beside him.

The women stayed to themselves emerging from their bedroom only for dinner. One of them appeared to be religious while the focus of the other was her daughter who visited weekly. Once while partaking of coffee with William he announced that he had been to jail on cocaine charges. He didn't seem to fit the type but then, I suppose, what is meant by this allusion. These then are some of the loose ends to the people surrounding me.

I sat down upon the bed and wrote a letter to the girls deliberately avoiding any explication of homelessness, jail, and finally this board and care. I told them, without wavering, that I longed to be with them but that my current job as a gardener wouldn't permit it yet. In a few months I would have the savings. In other words, I lied by omission and spared them of any troubling details.

We drove to the beach. I hadn't been there in a long while and its vastness, the pounding and hammering of the waves, and the smell of brine flooded my soul. While the others fished from the pier l took to the water to awaken me from my sedation. The cold water did, indeed, enliven me and my ears were cocked to hear the plaintive sound of the gulls. However, as I didn't wish to tamper with luck and drowned out at sea I soon released myself from the water's grasp.

At work that night I took to the book. Plunged without regret I became the servant of words once again. I was becoming close to the end and though I couldn't explain it there was a sadness to its conclusion. I was pleased with its exordium but I couldn't foresee an adequate closing. Good natured impressions abounded but there was nothing arbitrarily settled and so I shut the book and mused at the stars.

I began deliberating about the past, present, and future. Would anybody find in this book a slender morsel of humanity from one who had struggled amongst the throng of man and had been dutifully released? It was painful to think otherwise. Would Cupid answer me with Elaine? Again, it was painful to think otherwise. Was my book nothing more than a perversion of good taste, something to jeer at with disdain? Or, as has been related before, was it merely a generous dash of bitterly news that couldn't be digested? Would I be exonerated from any crippling terms or the general disquiet of its nature from premises to the conclusion? Were there concessions made which sacrificed the text or was there smooth sailing in the most vehement of expressions? Had my sensibilities been divested from the beginning or was there a fatalistic brew that couldn't be denied? I finally tore myself away from these unhealthy considerations and I arrived at an inescapable finish. Yes, tonight I would end this siege of words and with a little care bring my book to an end. Having obtained a typewriter it would only be a number of weeks before it was edited and typed for the publisher.

Six weeks, henceforth, I awoke from my sleep with my book shining so brightly. It, and the light

85

of day, were simply wonderful. No more skirling, no more skirmishes with ideas and words. It was over! Hopping on my scooter I took the long way to the post office, the sun shining on my back, and I delivered my parcel to the publisher of my first short story so long ago. I had good feelings, but then I always had, even in the rejected material.

I walked often and laughter was becoming more commonplace. I hadn't realized how dreary and introspective I had become and this recovery was acknowledged by nearly everyone. The pain in my heart was mending. But had the revisions to my book been thorough enough or had I botched it with such haste? In other words, had I trimmed its corpulence making it lean and inhabitable? Well, it wouldn't have me under the weather for today at least. No need to let a vein or sever an artery. In my distended mood I was as happy as a lark. It was, after all, a good natured try and I wouldn't have to mourn the early death of my novel no matter what success it might be lacking. With its completion it had been put to rest.

I sat down to write the girls in the midst of these thoughts denying them a good look at my exploits. Only later would it be a good time to divulge my many ignominious affairs. What would they think of my time homeless, my brief prison stay, and presently this board and care for the disabled? Why, I couldn't fathom it myself! In this connection, I stopped taking my medicine on the sly and I was rewarded by the alertness of my former self. I began to wonder what on earth was I doing here. The people and their habits were not only unnerving but unacceptable as well. Like automata they roamed the grounds, speechless and beaten down. I felt pity and sorrow for them but I couldn't very well express myself. Besides, it would only fall upon deaf ears. I found myself begging for more work to provide for my trip back East.

My thoughts of being published had surfaced once again and was leaking into my brain with exquisite precision. Soon, soon, I thought as I mopped the floor. But it began to be a sort of siege to my mind displacing it with obsession and rallying about me for my singular attention.

William and I took a break from the monotony of our chores. In a matter of weeks I would earn the money to make my escape from this ward though I wouldn't have much more than the cost of transportation and a few meals. I was getting more and more antsy as time went by. All that I now reflected upon was to be close to my beloved, Elaine. I thought of the first time that our eyes met and longed for the tenderness that was ours. No doubt, laughter, too, would abound. It, after all, was all that I had and the fondness of these memories had hitherto been my godsend for many troublesome nights. I told William this much and more as we had taken of one another's confidences. I discovered that he was on the brink of leaving himself as his lover's father was disenchanted with him. Evidently he would be returning home to the South where his family resided. He seemed as though he was fidgeting about and more talkative than usual and I wondered if he had partaken of some cocaine.

But despite his shortcomings I found him to be a kindred soul and I felt privileged to know him.

X

I wasn't truly expecting any grateful reply. Perhaps, I thought, the publishers had washed their hands of me altogether. That was why I let out a cry of elation, almost an inhuman cry, when I received it—the acceptance of *Tyranny and the Devil*, that is. So they hadn't forgotten me! I bounded clicking my feet, and rubbing my hands together. And I paused, with a great sigh, thanking providence for this redemption. Not only was it to be published but there was a handsome stipend and royalties to be delivered with time and the proper signatures. I felt like rubbing the news in the face of the prison doctor.

I took a stroll in the garden as if I was finally a free man. No longer would I ever doubt myself nor my veracity. I was almost foaming at the mouth when I sent off a note to Helen and Elaine, enclosing a photocopy of my letter of acceptance. My hands were shaking visibly and I almost began stammering with the postal worker. I wanted to shout at the world as if I was the only man alive to be published but I kept myself in check not wanting to be carted away as a madman or misfit. Should I tell you that they used the adjective "brilliant" to define my work?

From the train above the center of town I saluted The Greeter and reread the golden invitation from the girls to join them. Yes, above this nervous and choleric rant I was loved, and I began counting to fifteen.

PART TWO

I

I must renounce this chamber of horrors in my mind for I believe, beneath my feet, lay mortal bliss. What is more there is a prodigious gratitude few have known. Today I am as garrulous as a mockingbird, not partaking of sad and sorry explanations. I may have my head in the clouds but, oh, the wonder of it besieged by these phantasms, this delusional and devilish apparatus that keeps me hunting. This debacle and the scabrous insults have nearly come to pass. Instead I sit and wait. Perhaps for the company of one of my cronies on the train. One of them is a fat man, a decent sort, a fine fellow, and a generous soul, not given to prattle. His face is quite memorable. He is almost toothless and though I haven't spoken to him about it I must deduct that somewhere along his hard road he had them knocked out. Hence, he is the subject of some pity.

Once upon a time there was no peace, great or small. Presently freedom reigns. After all, I didn't invent it nor did I draw it from a hat. I've been over it, again and again. Still nothing washes, nothing figures. However, today there are but these clear horizons as I sit in the club car with other chipper pals taking in the glorious day. My mind is swimming like the clouds through the sky.

Long ago, on sleepless nights, and without my wits, I would mount iron steps, such as these on the train, to my bedroom with great trepidation. Still, I was convinced that despite such crossroads I would swing about. Such struggle was not without consequence but still with little effort arose the confounded images. Why, at one time, did I play so helpless, awaiting the pith of rage to pass. Now I hold up a dozen roses my dear friends. It is a walk in the park. In the meantime I discover myself the champion of first principles. Ah, but to quench my passions while poetry is daring me. Happiness, you see, is as absolute as oblivion. No longer do I rub my face in this self-imposed solitude. I try so hard, so very hard, and I am meanwhile not worthy of your ears without melancholy being dragged along with other dolorous terms. The muzzle that I wore before was now no more than an absurd mask. Mania, like ennui and inertia, has all but dispersed as has the suffering that had ransacked me. But nothing can happen out of the ordinary and this is paramount to my progress. I will not crow about such mischief. The power of the elite is at my doorstep. I feel it welling up inside of me even if it sometimes appears both rank and inelegant. I shall not, henceforth, speak ill of myself as before. Whatever bitter experiences pass my way I will not resign myself to such conquests though the presence sometimes of lame shadows and stillborn cries emerge unexpectedly. I shall continue on even if I hold up only gallows humor. In the stillness of the air I shall struggle and fight regardless of the cowardice I sometimes feel. My madness shall no longer make me run, trampling the flower beds, so to speak. Insults will no longer tempt me to hide. I will not grow uncommunicative nor as stifled as a mechanical body. Oh, the embrace and the moist kisses wandering shall renew me. Before there was nothing but mock heroics with which to abide. There was simply put the personification of

93

evil. Be that the truth or not I am idle in my affairs, anxious to be put to the test. Running at the mouth I have, nevertheless, no need to make others sore.

As for the streets there is but the noise of insanity. Nearly everybody there has been duped by the delusions of living forever. Thank the powers that be for the occasional comic interlude. Perhaps wearing socks on my hands I will make a puppet show at the park. Meanwhile, the wind is blowing up the dust in a tantrum. The frenzy of words is drawing me out, making of love a fatal consequence. Yes, wicked is sometimes the tempest of love but I refuse to be plunged into a deep despair. Nonetheless, my stage is made of straw, the audience mere puppets. Sometimes I will moan with the weight of this worry, lamenting the past not the present. But mine is not to fret for some form of enlightenment is sure to come, scattering the shadows. Even if my limited diction is the language of dwarves and a little lame I shall stand bemused more than stymied at these trespasses. No matter what the price I will become affectionately reckless and without equal. But I shall remain, always, the

perfect gentleman. As for me, "I was born many!"
[Socrates]

My temples ache as I triumph in my struggles. To crush the agonies that present themselves, I must endure. Who are they, after all, but harmless tit mice? The immense pain of the recent past shall pale while I am being delivered, coming out of darkness. Fine, we shall all croak together. The prince of darkness and his odious crimes shall find me in an austere light, no longer guilty of former charges. Nor do I care a fiddlestick for their exploits of me.

Oh, these idle hours! Nevertheless, at other times don't you see, I was steeped in it. That is, the lightening and thunder of it all striking me into an awkward pose. Above these racing silhouettes, on the edge of calamity, the seeds of abomination bourgeoning in the backstage, surely you must see that I must insist on my redemption. A bad ending, a good ending, let us hope for the best.

Today I will shorn my locks and take a shave, weary of the journey. Meanwhile, I have employed every means for the battles that are sure to ensue.

Is there nobody to hear my cries? What prophecies and legerdemain shall pass my way? I don't know how to read any longer, nor do I know how to sing. I must derive from the winter sun each and every latitude. I am both sorrowful and curious, but merely to silence myself is not the answer. So I continue to write haunted by those that have forsaken me. Vigorous of limb I must tread the waters and this war with words. But what must I do to induce this scrimmage? Am I painting myself into a corner?

And so time has come to pass. It is nearly Christmas and about one year since I have seen the gals. Their loyalty is breathtaking. My transportation is winding down the last slopes like a toy train. I am giddy with anticipation and I have managed to buy them a few simple gifts. The town seems to be bustling in honor of my visit and everywhere there seems to be indications of spiritual warmth. The ride is over and I can see the girls waving deliriously by my cabin door and furiously I return their salute. Tears began to overwhelm me. I have scotched my old life and I am prepared to bound into my new one. My ride has given me new considerations and prospects. Depending upon my royalties I might well have a chance to buy a home as the prices are not as steep as out West. There will be plenty of time to coax the girls into staying with me for I wouldn't venture staying alone in my new home. Perhaps we might live upstairs and have a thrift store downstairs as before. But we mustn't rush into anything though, I must admit, there is a fever burning inside me to take care of my loves. However, I felt my urges to write ebbing away as before. What new branch of creation would summon me forth? And the thought occurred to me, could one be happy and write? After all marriage wasn't out of the question. There shouldn't be any doubt that I would not turn away and ignore my hunger for such a union. My feelings were invincible. But when all has been said and done, was I merely a delinquent at love?

Helen and Elaine are in good form. Kisses are passed around. I noted that they referred to me as little Shakespeare. Meanwhile I am on top of the world. I am going to my new home where I may

97

live and breathe comfortably among good company. There is no gainsaying it, I thrust forth without reservations. A good meal was on the agenda as well as an abundance of conversation. In fact, I hadn't spoken to anybody but for William as much as the hour that is passing by. Why should I marvel at these junctures but that they were perhaps rare with me. Besides, we had a lot of catching up to do and we were doing it with great and joyous haste. You might say that we were lit from both ends.

Apparently the tides of their lives were almost as imaginative as what I had endured. But not quite so, I realized, as confessions began to spill out of me. However it was precisely this magnanimity they were showing that endeared me to them from the beginning. Yes, they had a whopping sense of humor and made light of the most appalling circumstances. I had almost forgotten the comic aspect of things and presently I was entirely without remorse. Nothing seemed to upset them from my scroll of bad adventures, but for me this town was a far cry from the sleepy town we had once shared. The truth be known I was a little apprehensive. In other words, the traffic of people and cars were astounding. Had it been another smaller town I might have more easily acquiesced. Still it was too premature to make such judgments and my gracious company made it difficult to think otherwise of these climes. This then was my jury and peers, I summarized with good tidings, and I found my patience growing by leaps and bounds. Given time this atmosphere would, no doubt, become absorbed and congenial as it had come to pass with Helen and Elaine. I was certainly not arrogant enough to breach these good times and I was standing in good favor with those whom embraced me.

Rarely do I encourage conversation from this inwardness. But today I am succoring the marrow of life. Quiet dreams have come my way. No longer am I dissuaded from my purpose, whatever purpose that might be. By virtue of these leading ladies I must ask may I sustain my wits and not express my mirthless charms. After all, they seem to be able to see right through me and anybody so

99

inclined, well, I would have thought that they would have vanished. Perhaps it is only timing, my dear fool, I counseled. Perhaps the weather that has crossed my path is far beyond my understanding. The fire that before raged was instinct. Was I to be robbed any longer of my drives. What surprises lay ahead in the shadows? What is still distinguishable in the palette of this netherworld? Oh, these wonders, will they never cease. This last purge of writing, it has taken me by the gut and promised me everything! This mine was deep and surely to flourish in the days ahead. Perhaps the impenetrable has come to pass. What is left to define the man?

The crowds milling around, the wheelchairs, the laughter, and the bric-a-brac seemed all so determined. But was a veil falling before us? For something inside me said, "You are making a dreadful mistake and you will pay for it."

II

A taxi was waiting by the curb. For whatever reasons I am shaking like a leaf! The girls enter first. "What nemesis are you looking for?" ask my darlings, laughing all the while. "The shock of it all," I rejoin without bitterness. After you've gone quite mad there is nowhere to go, I think to myself.

We entered squalid surroundings, a low rent district. How does one treat this? I ask. Goodness forbid, if you fall into the wrong hands, I mused. This smear on my reputation, *Tyranny and the Devil* will soon pass, I console myself. "Nothing more than a madman," I can hear them all say. My more unkind critics would like to see the death of me, to be sure. But I wouldn't permit them to see the dissolution of my faculties, no matter how dreadful the consequences. But it's understandable, you're tired, I tell myself. I've never maligned anyone in this circus of manners before and it went on without a snag. Why shouldn't I be able to carry on even with the detriment of their criticism. But I am so wary that I write under an alias. To be sure I didn't want to fuel their distasteful run of the mouth that had me coming and going. No, a lucky man was I! Blind laughter is engaging me with its great maw. Delicate is that of my scrutiny, delicate is that of my legion of memory.

The birds are chirping without let and the gals are sharing a shower. Even in the cold I am usually inclined to bathe in the sea. Whatever emotion rides me I must continue on. To cheat, lie, and swindle was my lot. But today I am limping, hobbling to my desk for more insults. I am suffering from tendonitis and I don't know why.

At the market place things are bustling and I lumber down the lane, as if a broken man. "Oh, golden one, the writer in me, you bore me!" I shout inside.

Later the darkness falls like a steel trap. The dog and I are scampering through the brush behind our house. It is our joyous habit. At home the breeze is having its way blowing through the windows of my study. No sooner do I puzzle over these shadows of Morpheus that I grow flush with its message: "Triumph, triumph," I hear "them" say.

"You must write now," they badger me. For what unfathomable reason I acquiesce to this mood. I am as afraid as a child during a nightmare. I float helplessly wanting merely to bust out of this joint. But only at times am I this victim of unhappiness, a visitant of unhealthy climes. Are the gals aware of my plight? For it is true that in their company I am soundly resurrected. That which grieves me walks out the door. In fact, I am conscious of moods as different as night and day. Let it suffice to say that they are devouring me. In addition to this memories of jail and the board and care were raising their demented heads. Something told me if I wasn't careful I might well be evicted by Helen and Elaine. Strangely enough this met with little resistance for in the back of my mind I was sometimes, perhaps, relishing solitude.

My wallet was fat with money for the first time in my life and my wealth was increasing with royalties from my book. What is more, I was well on my way in my second novel from which I expected an even more generous salary. But something was counseling me to take the easy path as

things unfolded. And to this mandate did I propose to venture unscathed and free. Meanwhile we
were, all three of us, scheduled today to meet with
the realtor about housing. In this regard I noticed
that the more money that I had the more parsimo-
nious I became. Besides if I didn't watch my back I
might well not only be unhappy with the terms of
the company but robbed of a good portion of money to boot. But were such thoughts from the inside
looking out or the outside looking in? Could I
manage alone or was it necessary that I have company to frighten away these crows that would
sometimes burden me. On top of this I was always
painfully shy. No, I must be noble in my cause.
The girls, after all, were responsible for saving my
life and giving me joy and they deserved more than
these paltry reservations. Sometimes, I must confess, I wrongly assume that I am the fish eye of all
humanity. I am reminded that one must make sac-
rifices. Indeed, one must make some form of
atonement and restitution for the things worthy in
life. But every time that I turn around it would
seem, from faint whisperings, that there are legions

of my enemy kicking and crying. I deserve the bronze star for these many trespasses. I have cried my heart out and for what? Ah, but today my heart is singing. My scavengers are on the run! There is no need for bravery to shine on such days. Good lord, I have been hoodwinked, deceived beyond measure, and I still refuse to crawl. So I must shine upon these days. I must take my life into my own hands.

The realtor was digging her nails into us at every prospective house that we visited. We were all a little put off by this until there came what seemed to be a promising match to our expectations. It was a two story dwelling perfect for a thrift store and the zoning laws were permissible for such an arrangement. After a brief consultation among ourselves we agreed that it was suitable for our purposes. Eventually the papers were signed and we found ourselves the proud owners of both a thrift shop and lodging. Peanuts, the dog, seemed to enjoy the small garden in the back and we, too, enjoyed planting many flowers in the yard that suffered from neglect. Meanwhile I had converted the spare room upstairs into a cozy study. Writing was taking shape and Helen and Elaine seemed to be floating on air. I was becoming chummy with my second and third books and in this regard my expectations seemed to soar. Still I was not altogether capable of forgetting my spotted past and the less kind critics, I noted, merely thought of me as a sick poet. But without paying too much attention I thumbed my nose at these devils. Come dinner, when the pugilism of writing had ceased, I would frolic in the backyard barbecuing for an outdoor dinner and sharing stories with the gals. Things could not be better, I thought.

There is a harbor nearby and it is my habit to visit her in dawn or dusk when the light is most advantageous to a form of serenity. There I would relish a twilight state nearly giving up the ghost while seeking such solace. While, as a child, it had precipitated similar feelings. I was still that child but for a few gray hairs and in my heart I was at the beacon of my life, chanting and glorifying life the best I could. My wishes didn't, after all, imitate a wintry landscape. No, I was too happy most of the time to settle for such a surrender. But now it is time to return home for more glad tidings. I am these days on the verge of a happiness of which most never dreamed and the girls were never guilty of finding fault with me.

And so it was another evening entertaining one another with the events of the day as well as listening to the gals sing and play folk music on their guitars until the late hours. It always astonished me that they would include me in their affairs from the most trivial to the most significant. I was always quick to let them know my unbridled gratitude. They were, indeed, my angels!

III

However, before we continue with this mirth of place I must tell you that the house was sometimes haunted. In this connection I discovered the relics of writing in an old cupboard in the study. He wasn't entirely without talent and I chose to let Helen and Elaine in on this ghostly bit of news. They were quite taken aback as was I. On top of this there were unaccountable sounds but for the deeds of apparitions. The substance of this old manuscript featured three distinct persons, a man and two women such as we were. Add to this that the man was a writer and the two women worked in a clothing store and you have the irony of this story. As if this wasn't enough, all three of us were visited nocturnally with indistinguishable whispers. To fortify our spirits we all slept in the same bed. Gaining strength from our proximity helped us to quietly sleep. Meanwhile, Peanuts would occasionally bark without provocation. And as if this wasn't enough one of the strings on the guitar would snap giving us a jolt of reality. Henceforth sometimes our little house was merely a shattered dream and our presence a nuisance to these evanescent intrusions. What tasks must follow to disinter and banish these haunting unrealities? We wondered. We, after all, didn't wish to succumb to the powers of their trespasses. And so together we would prepare an elixir of sorts to this demonizing. Oh, but how disgraceful was this bandaging of wounds for we would indulge regularly in a few

gin and tonics to expel the tactile hallucinations
that were even more troublesome than the whispers. In part it reminded me of homelessness and
jail and all the irreverent deeds done to me. More
often than not we would seek refuge at the harbor,
picnicking to save ourselves from any of the weak
bantering at the house. But this could not last, I
told myself. Surely there must be a remedy to
chase away these devils hard at work. Their feroci-
ty seemed to appear nocturnally. Daylight hours
were largely governed by our own choosing. There
was nothing so contemptible as their appearance as
we would gasp at their ill manners. All at once we
were entwined at their beck and call. Nevertheless
there were no other quandaries preventing us from
smooth sailing. Give into these apparitions, no
never! Perhaps the day would come when we
would befriend them, thus making them impotent
to us. For despite their contemptuousness we
couldn't be duped nor cozened by their artifice.

Among their murmurs sloping down the
staircase we would often try to commit them so
that we might more readily distinguish their con-

tent. But despite the despicable nature of these hidden beasts there was a merrier side. For during the hours that I wrote in my study I would often swear that they were helping me to limp along, giving me a nudge here and there, particularly when I became buckled up by my own caprice.

I was presently completing my third novel and there was no gainsaying it I was making good and great progress on a daily basis. Rather than curtailing my efforts the ghosts seem to propel me in a forward fashion making me almost feel as if I was plagiarizing in their presence. What is more, as the day waned, I would find myself penning notes in the sea breeze at the quay, quite enraptured by the solitude at my shoulders. At such times my soul was invited to pay my respects to nature forgetting all the while the ghosts and goblins. But upon my return home I would often reacquaint myself with this double of mine, and his lost manuscript in the cupboard. It would appear that he was well versed in matters of speech and wasn't shy at expressing both his mirth and despair regarding his condition. Eye to eye, so to speak, I could well imagine the situation in which he found himself and I secretly robbed him of some of his more poignant remarks. What was good enough for him was good enough for me, I delighted. And so I would pinch here and there a distinct perception that found its way into my own constitution. After all, why should I not take this opportunity to give life to this lost prose, unveiling a new face to his efforts? Had he been here in person we might have gotten along famously. To be sure there was some form of intimacy between our impressions, impressions that, at a glance, appeared to be a mystification and simplicity of similar objectives. At other times his manuscript was shy of holding the beauty of his other commentary and his direction perplexed me. Perhaps he was guilty of being the recipient of former tenants himself and their ghostly presence as were we. However, there was only minimal dialogue to this affect. And yet, what could I say, it was there glowing in the darkness of his verse. The mention of nightly mutterings haunting the household and upsetting the rhythms of behavior of himself and his two lovers.

111

The study room was dusty with a tumble of manuscripts and the transparencies from the gauze of the delicate lace curtain. As night approached I lit a candle. The whispers were inaudible but lay on the edge of consciousness like an actor backstage rehearsing his lines. It was enough to be horrified by these newborns and I sat amidst the raw substance of a dream, the properties of which I was well familiar. They were dissimulating with the cunning of a fox and I was madly impressed. But why look for justification beneath this patina of mutterings? There were none! And so, mellow at my post, I let them pass through me. Sometimes, quite ironically, it was a challenge and objective as good as good gets. At other times they seemed to beg me to stay seated at their stage and without so much as a whimper. At such time I would write letters that made no sense. Far and wide the voices roamed like a nomadic tribe seeking out quarters that were not hostile to their regime. Meanwhile, second to none, I felt my patience grow and I was clearly the benefactor of their meanderings while they poured out as through a sieve.

112

"Am I the man of the mountain?" I would query. "For I am as mellow as the soft, dusk light," I mused. Yet, how should I say, I must grow myself up and tear my way through it. The wanderer I shall be with some form of divine reminiscence. History is being made, thought I, not suffering from the sole conviction that the voices were altogether benign. But once you are used up you must run from the dim shadows, the hounds being everywhere and nowhere alike. So with this duplicity I departed my study to consult with the gals on my latest correspondence with these ghostly imps. I must admit many times I would frighten them with my latest communion when the voices became friendly or even amorous. What was transported by this breeze of sound flitting through my skull was uncertain in the last analysis. But it surely demanded closer inspection, if not outright scrutiny, to deter them from intruding into my actions and affairs with the girls.

At the worst this swine of the netherworld seemed to ingratiate itself as the sea runs far and wide, destroying the beauty of the bay and ransacking one's mind though I was far from home. The transplantation of these elements to other places made me wince at the potency of their transgressions. I began to wonder if my former voices out west were somehow infused with the presence of the ghosts in our home. It was difficult to illuminate the several possibilities and the beauty of the girls had my disposition warming considerably with their charms and kindness. Henceforth I was saved, more than once, by their presence alone. If I wished to write in these troubled times the voices must perish. They were, too often, making a mockery of my efforts. Whether or not I should seek out some form of medication was a plausible remedy, I thought. However, a few glasses of wine often softened these intrusions and permitted me to make love whereas the drug's sedation would make one nearly impotent.

I was, it is true, torn between pleasures of the flesh and the occurrences of these menacing whispers. Nevertheless for now things were tolerable and they were not severe enough to warrant a change. My writing and sex was still greatly satisfying. Particularly with the situation of making love to both women at the same time. At least the fire in my loins was true as was the fire of my writing. No, these voices were only a mild keepsake nursing themselves on the spring rain with summer on the horizon. We were merely children at play not wishing to disturb the cadence of our affairs nor breaching the tempo of our relations. The voices were, for the most part, chameleons seeking their own path. In spite of these dwarves swimming in the air I was wont to open the window, the window that would permit their entrance into my study, perhaps, shaking up the peace of our former tenants. The itinerant, what would my sketches reveal to the next boarder?

In the distance I could make out Helen and Elaine wearing their scarves. They looked like two frolicking gypsies walking arm in arm. Tonight we would go dancing. Yes, once a week we would find ourselves at a club shedding our inhibitions and the ghosts alike. This would always engender a smile from the girls, shuffling my feet, as in a comical skit. But my dancing had improved thanks

115

to the girls efforts at home, readying me for public display. At first I was self conscious but with time I began to warm to the situation and lost the buckram of my intellect or what was left of it. In fact I found myself no longer lumbering about and stamping my feet. No, instead I was gliding and creating smiles in my midst. Namely the smiles of the girls. We were often bent over laughing at my antics and the more I clowned around the better time we had of it. I was coming into my own realizing how happiness was finally mine. No doubt I was the envy of other men as I paraded around with two women. Sometimes we were forced to leave early because of their unwelcome intrusions while at other times we closed down the club late at night.

At home we would play music continuing with our dancing and shedding our clothes we would find ourselves in the nude embracing one another until we found the bed. Oftentimes the girls would roll some marijuana trying to coax me into participation. But I was adamant with my rejection not caring for the paranoia that accompanied it. Meanwhile the girls would become riotous with laughter making good natured fun of me and spanking my butt. Sometimes I would secretly record their mischief only to play it back to them the next morning. Unaware of such antics they would cringe, then laugh to beat hell. That was then, this is now!

IV

It was my birthday and we prepared ourselves for a picnic at the bay. At such times they would ask me to read to them some of my current manuscript. In this regard they were a bastion to my creativity. For their intentions were frank and honorable and I often felt relieved when they would applaud a passage or two. A man may dream but it would fall short of my happiness. They were forever making appeals to my inventions and giving birth to new crossroads. Yes, love was the reply to the gravest of problems and it was the little things that were so permeable to joy. In spite of my troublesome paths I was advancing to a

117

higher ground and I was relishing each moment as I climbed.

My second and third books had been sent to my editor and the publishing house. I could sense the publisher rubbing his hands together with glee. It may have been my own conceit but I truly felt that the second book was better than the first and worse than the third. In other words I was improving by leaps and bounds. What is more, I was attracting quite a following. It would appear that there were many drawn to and beckoned by some of these writings about the edge of madness. No doubt they were making a mockery of me in classes of introductory psychology. Reflections of this two edged sword made me feel like a fool second to none. In fact, a few weeks before I had rejected an invitation to speak at one of the many colleges nearby. I preferred signing books despite the exposure and public relations of speaking to a university.

My books were beginning to assume the proportions of a novella. Rather naturally came this form of endeavor and I seemed to be programmed into the space of approximately one hundred and some odd pages. Anything more from me was simply poor manners. It was only a matter of fastening onto a topic and then skipping stones. At least, at the inception, there was no end to be seen.

But as my audience grew so did the intrusions into my private life. My capacity to conform to the push and pull of my reading public was next to nil and I found myself disconnecting the telephone and turning a cold shoulder to my mail. Locked in my little study I would find myself swept away with the subject at hand and, accordingly, I would mark the calendar with the due dates of each chapter. Such an agenda impelled me to conform to a necessary time frame and I practiced it religiously!

At lunch hour we would gather for a meal and then take a brief nap. Occasionally I would help the girls shelve books. However, I would often find myself perusing them with a studied interest and the gals would laugh and carry on about my infatuations. Often I would lose myself completely for an hour at a time, making remarks in my notebook, only later to be gathered like so much

119

dross for the fireplace. But my favorite hour was the hour that I would permit myself to play in the garden. There I would plant new flowers which I would later watch as they grew and blossomed.

One day per week I would indulge myself opening my mail and corresponding with a chosen few. It should go without saying that I was often disturbed by some of these letters. There were letters that either portrayed mental illness as paradigm of wisdom or, contrarily, a crime that needed punishment. Though they were both afflictions that deracinated me I found myself making brief replies to others unaware of how they would view them. Still I remained steadfast in my limited time. Yes, for the most part they were no more than letters of sheer nonsense and reprimands or undue praise of my work.

As time wore on circumstances began to change. With my popularity it sometimes seemed as though my name was a household word. Book sales began to soar. As odious as it sounded my public appearances, though dreaded, had come to claim me. I had a sinking and foreboding feeling.

My publisher, you see, was quick to point out that I needed to do a little spadework to augment even more the sale of my books. To his mind I was shrugging off my task and my duties as an author. Money began to get the upper hand, to rule me, and to chase away the more simple and delightful times at home. Thus my publisher, who stood to profit as well, had booked me on a circuit or tour of a few different states. Reaching as far as the West coast my itinerary loomed in front of me bringing back harsh realities. To this end I could feel my primitive self emerging. I must banish my timorous and nervous disposition, my self consciousness that ran from my feet to my scalp. The most displeasing aspect and onus to my affairs was that my reputation was beginning to become synonymous with schizophrenia itself. I should have been aware of such nonsense, I scolded myself, and readied my replies to this effrontery.

After speaking at a large university I began to form the opinion that no man was worth this preoccupation and scrutiny. The questions appeared to be nothing more than an interrogation into my personal life. Some of them were even mean-spirited and manifold with barbs meant to induce my fall into a state of dissolution and chaos.

As I hemmed and hawed at these questions I found myself increasingly disoriented and on the brink of fainting. Sometimes, the truth be known, I couldn't wait to disappear and lay down in my forlorn hotel far away from all seeing eyes. At other times it was rather harmonious to speak with these less hostile students and faculties. Still, the more crowded the arena the more agitated I became. The bookstores were much more to my liking, not practicing the asperity of the larger crowds. I took to them with a relish after having my mind ransacked at a larger university. Anyway, my loyalties were back East with the girls and I would visit them by telephone on a daily basis. This was as nourishing as circumstances would have it and I cherished their voices in my lonely hotel. Fortunately, the weather permitting, I would indulge myself with a swim. I had long ago given up on preparing a lecture with pertinent notes and I languished in an indolent manner at night hoping that the extemporaneous would work comfortably as opposed to the script. Sometimes, off the cuff, I would surprise myself, tunneling through the text, as it were. But largely these times were few and I would awkwardly stare at the rafters wondering what on earth I was doing here. No, my life hadn't prepared me for this public beating. I was still the young boy sauntering down the bridal path, whistling a merry tune. A few, but good friendships, and an appetite for the arts was my mainstay. Had anyone broached me about being published at a later stage I would have thought that they were quite mad.

The time was soon approaching when the last leg of my trip would be consummated. My cowering self would vanish and I would be saved from any mismanaged replies. But I don't wish to stop here for, to my surprise, the crowds despite my hedging manner would often applaud my efforts. I suppose to save me from falling and to enhance my self worth as my diffidence was very much apparent. After all, my books were of such a personal nature that it was inescapable to avoid a confessional attitude. It happened quite often that the students and others viewed me as an adventure-some and romantic ideal. There was a fondness for them to elevate me above my lonely station and they, sometimes, did this without reservation.

Thus I scampered about the many universities and bookstores playing my hand and inviting their magnanimity to flourish. For without their kindness I was left to mutter to myself and to fade into a sort of oblivion. My introduction into these affairs was the first university to which I spoke. The very first thing that they said aloud was for me to speak up. This derailed me from my script such that I could no longer follow it but instead I began speaking about my life. In so doing I was getting dangerously close to my struggling self, wading in a bog of disclosures. By the end of it all I was ready to burst at the seams. What is more their questions often invoked lies on my part, not wishing to admit some of my follies. I almost began to splutter from the text no longer capable of dissection and coherence. Yes, most of the time I resorted to reading from my books as an easy way out. Had there been, I wished, only a few people with which to chat, but no, that were sometimes at least one hundred souls and their looks were hard.

I tell you I was unable to pursue many lines of questioning. I was reminded that such venom had cost me years of my life. That is the refusals of my books and stories by the publishers. I cringed at the heart of the matter. For what did some of them want but for me to burn in hell while others lay in compassion. To the latter I was in my element and succumbed with great ease. Sometimes I would break away into humor. Yes, I was in need of striking out, expunging the true record of my autobiography. Surely somebody must see this coming, the foul circumstances of confessing too much and victimized where these sharks sensed blood.

Meanwhile at the hotel I was understandably tired. I would invariably speak to the girls. It would appear that the ghosts were on the rampage and, accordingly, they had locked my study door. I laughed at this out loud comparing these trifles to my own drudgery with these classrooms.

But presently outside my door there was a breeze and the Chinese lanterns were swaying as were the brilliant placards and bunting. Soon I would be reunited with my lovers and Peanuts, the dog. My publisher called to inform me that my books were doing more than well in Europe. Yes, presumably the sale of my books had shot up dramatically while I was away. The only thorn was that the publisher would eventually want me to go abroad to elevate my sales as I was now doing in the states. Perhaps, at times, I might have to compromise but for now we, my publisher and I, struck an accord to these logistics. Thus, there was a brighter side to my future and appropriately I took to dancing in my hotel room, dreaming of the girls and our approaching rendezvous.

And so by train I boarded one last time to find some sort of peace at my final colloquium. I was feeling quite buoyant, vibrant, and alive. Yes, I was on top of the world and I could no longer see a down side. As a result I thrived at the many questions, my replies being quick and succinct, my manners of delivery impeccable. Should somebody have compared this to my first outing they would be astounded at the favorable comparison.

126

Mendacity no longer played a part and I was as candid and garrulous as I was at the book signings. Perhaps this had to do with the proximity of my departure or it was a healthy response to my European sales but the ease in which I participated was worthy of my finest efforts. For now I was ecstatic at my return home and I couldn't write a word. The gals and our home were the only thoughts that I had.

V

When I returned home I first went downstairs to the thrift shop. There I found the girls rummaging through some of the copious clothing. They were expecting me but that didn't curtail our excitement. We hung the closed sign on the door and tramped upstairs to our kitchen to have a bite to eat. I filled their heads with the tales of my journey, making some of them up for our amusement. However, we couldn't wait to get to the bedroom and so I postponed telling them of my plan to vacation in the tropics. Later, after sexual exhaustion, I broached the subject. They were excited with my proposal. We took out a map of various tropical islands and decided on one that appealed not only to a sense of beauty but good cuisine as well. Contrary to these colder parts I would be able to swim with free abandon and catch some sun. As in my youth I would be left to indulge my senses. But that had been so long ago and so many bridges had been crossed. Presently I was entertaining a fat bankroll and a rising reputation. And let us not forget the girls and their source of joy. No, the money wasn't everything but it certainly freed us up to indulge our fancies.

I took the mail upstairs and entered my study. It was even more dusty though it was locked up, with the window closed. There was mail from my editor and publisher which I first opened. It would appear that there were many questions arising from the translation of my books in Europe and Asia. Invitations were sent out to visit me sometime in the next few weeks following my vacation. How my life had turned around was quite unfathomable.

But for now I was luxuriating on an island far from home. The girls looked so inviting in their French bikinis. Their bronze skin was radiating beauty and when they emerged from bathing in the sea they took the breath from me. So fond of the water and the light were we that we often ate on the beach. To this end there were a few barbecues turning out chicken, with bread and fruit in abundance. In the evening we would dance to our hearts content. The girls in their summer frocks and generous smiles I would twirl under the night sky until I was spent.

Our departure home would surely leave us with tears in our eyes so adaptable to this pleasure was our habitus. Though my mind was not exactly teeming with thoughts I managed to dictate a few notes to Helen and Elaine awaiting me with pen and paper. To their eyes they only resembled inanities but to mine they represented arrivals and departures for my prose to flourish. I was becoming anxious for the delivery of my next two books and to this end I, again, used the girls as a mirror to my reading public. Soon these novellas would be born from such idle chatter.

It occurred to me that at sometime in the future I might run dry and I would have to turn my face from my endeavors of writing. Nonetheless, for now, I could breach my inventions with some abruptness, finding exuberance at each performance. There was no need to fret about a future nobody could see. There was no need for circumstances that would negate my will. Yes, I was headstrong about this authorship and my publication had swung about to include several countries and a few continents as well.

In the sea the girls would climb my shoulders and spout water. This could last for nearly an hour before we sought refuge beneath our umbrella. Afterwards we would nap or take a trip to one of the many clothing shops. There I would take great delight in purchasing lovely dresses for them. Meanwhile, back on the beach, I would often become unnerved by the many photographers and camcorders selecting us as their target. The girls only laughed while I found it rather annoying.

One of them came so close, zooming in on us, that I had to chase him off. But in the end they were relentless. Here there were disadvantages of having to protect the girls and not knowing if I could pull it off. I was no lion but I had to play the pugilist occasionally when I was homeless. Using my wits more than my brawn I had managed to survive thus far. Still it was cumbersome being challenged by potential suitors and I often felt myself puffing up to do battle. Yes, I was, I suppose, their stallion and they were my mares and I took it upon myself to be the lion if need be. There was no denying it fencing with these devils was all that I could do. However, often we must have appeared to be no more than the meekness of violets in the hot sun. But then with renewed vigor I would scare away these birds, all and sundry.

Once, while swimming we had become the victims of a theft. Nothing worth anything was stolen, merely three pairs of sunglasses, but it infuriated me nevertheless. In this connection we agreed that somebody should always stay with our belongings.

131

The next day while playing Frisbee a dog approached us with its owner. It bore an uncanny resemblance to Peanuts and we took turns petting him, homesick for the first time. We all began to converse about our little homestead wondering what on earth the ghosts were up to. At supper that evening we, all three of us, sunk into a mild despondency. No doubt due to the dog and the ghost stories. It was true that we were all homebodies and we cherished our own turf. A broad and disagreeable silence began to engulf us. It wasn't until later that we resumed our sense of humor.

I decided that the next day I would go scuba diving. Despite my invitation and my coaxing the girls were not interested. So I embarked upon my voyage with a small group of men and women. I was quite anxious to visit the coves and sea life of flora and fauna. However, I missed sharing this beauty with my lovers, and my adventure suffered from their absence.

When I returned to the beach I took notice of their towels and umbrella were there but there wasn't a trace of them to be seen. They didn't appear to be in the water and I sought without success for an explanation. Part of my fear was justified as we had all agreed that we wouldn't leave our belongings alone on the beach. I noticed, too, that their new sunglasses lay upon their towels. As I strolled toward the rocks at the end of the shore I began to cringe for their fate, my imagination giving birth to countless sources of anxiety and repugnant episodes. My mind wouldn't cease from its hideous wanderings and I felt as though I was on the verge of a seizure. I began trotting down the strand of sand toward a nearby hut where food was being served up. Finally, there at a small table, I espied them sitting calmly and sucking at their ice creams oblivious of my presence. Abruptly I shook the fear that had seized me, pretending not to show worry at which they would surely laugh. Meanwhile I was panting from having run a fair distance and I explained to them that I had run for exercise. They merely looked at me with mischievous smiles and began to laugh. I had broken one of my sandals and I suppose that I looked quite comical. If

133

they only knew the extent of my worry they would be drowning in tears of laughter, I thought.

It was now our last day and at the behest of the girls we were to go fishing. Of course the boat left quite early but we were wide awake with great expectations of the catch. My parents never took me fishing and I guess you could say that it was all new to me. The girls were only children when their folks took them fishing and often they would spend the entire day at sea. As I said it was all very new to me and the instructions were daunting. I became seasick with the rocking of the boat but it was just as well for I couldn't bait a hook nor cast a line. The girls, being a little tom-boyish, were having an easy time of it but were having difficulty teaching me the ropes. At home we all had base-ball gloves and we would play together in the backyard. We were, in fact, polished in our per-formances. But this was a different task and I was falling behind while Helen and Elaine were catch-ing fish left and right. I never knew that it was so easy to produce tears from my clumsiness but the gals were absolutely weeping with good cheer. No doubt this was due to fatuous behavior on my part. They began to jeer at me calling me Buster Keaton and I succumbed to being the object of their jests.

While picking up our key at the front desk I was given a letter. As only the dog keeper, my editor, and my publisher knew of my whereabouts I was certain it was one of them. The return address proved to show that it was my editor. Apparently it was his opinion that we meet soon to review my last two novellas. To this effect I sent a message that he stay at our home rather than a hotel. The girls agreed to this and, as I was getting antsy to return to work, I pledged to be ready by the end of the week. I merely needed a few days to acclimate myself, I told him. We both agreed that being available in person was paramount and so it was the date and address had been posted and soon I would meet personally with Jonathan, my editor.

That night, sunburned and fatigued, we climbed into bed early and dreamed the dreams of the dead. On the plane reading the newspaper I was shocked to see my name on the best selling list. Jonathan had mentioned that there was a surprise waiting for me but I had no idea that it would come in this form. The girls and I were ecstatic and we toasted one another to beat the band.

Before returning home we stopped off at the dog sitters to pick up Peanuts. He was overjoyed with our arrival and as we picked him up to cuddle he let out a stream of urine so excited was he. This nuisance only endeared him to us that much more. When we reached home I took him for a jaunt through the chaparral. This he loved more than the backyard and at home we fed him the supper of his life. One could tell that he was worried the first few days fearing our departure without him again. Meanwhile the ghosts, who had lately become so very friendly, were at it again. This time the games had been staged in my study. I couldn't remember if I had shut the window but it was now open and papers were strewn over the entire floor in disarray. This only served to make us laugh and tickle one another. That night, in great contrast to the tropics, there was a sudden, cold storm and cozy in bed we all agreed that it was lovely to be home.

136

VI

In the distance there was the ring of chimes. I had begun cooking breakfast when Jonathan arrived. The girls awoke and there were introductions made. After a lively conversation and cleaning our plates Jonathan and I dismissed ourselves to go to the study.

My last book, *The Mangroves* was the first subject of the day. According to him it was one of my best books to date. The main character was quite eccentric but an eminently memorable and honorable portrait ensued. Suddenly my sadness appeared. I felt like weeping as if a child. I told him that I was being washed away in publicity. He counseled me that these were the hurdles I would have to jump. I resumed with my thoughts that I had come so far, literally from the gutter, and I could see myself in these passages a lost man. He continued with generous blandishments describing my feats at writing as praiseworthy. Meanwhile I felt as if my true self had been sacrificed and forsaken. However, with his heaps of approval, my tears gave way to inspiration. No, I wasn't divorced from my muses. I wasn't used up yet. We were making good strides. With most of his criticism I agreed and we attacked it on all fronts. What is more it was encouraging speaking face to face, particularly with one so admirably possessed with good sense and the love for a lean text. Despite this loving attention my critics were beginning their siege and there was no end in sight. Nevertheless I wasn't without my resources and here Jonathan's words about the demands of authorship, including ignoring some of one's critics, rang true.

After a productive morning we set out for the bay where the sanction of the birds as they stood sentry befriended us. I had taken with me some of the foreign correspondence sent to me by Chad, my publisher. The news about Paris first caught my attention. I had visited there as a young man, poor in dollars, rich in spirit. I was deeply aware of its many charms. As it turned out Jonathan, too, had traveled there in his youth. Apparently he had always wanted to sculpt and seeing the Rodin museum only increased his hunger that much more. To this day he had created such art in his spare time succeeding only in an amateurish exhibition if one was to accept his modesty. The thought occurred to me that we could both share in an adventure to France as well as Italy, England, and the Netherlands. They had all made appeals to me of speaking engagements and book signings. Having company conferred to me the courage that it would take to bring this off.

And thus we began our correspondence through Chad to make the necessary arrangements on our behalf. By this time next month we would both board a plane for Paris, then we would train to other parts of continental Europe, and finally we would visit London.

We opened a bottle of champagne and brought it downstairs to the thrift shop to share with the gals. They were excited for me, particularly having company on my long voyage, company that would give me much needed strength among the hardships of being scrutinized. Soon I excused myself to make brunch for everyone. I ambled upstairs thinking, with the flush given me by the champagne, that I would soon be visiting Paris where I had been overjoyed in my youth. Humming and whistling I went about preparing the meal and setting the table. I went back downstairs and found them all laughing. For a moment I thought that it might be at my expense but I soon banished the thought and announced that it was lunchtime. I seemed to have cut their conversation short and I felt mildly humiliated and even guilty of intruding in their affairs. After all there had been no other visitors to speak of since our arrival here. Perhaps the girls were starved for affection. I must admit I felt not a little jealous of their intimacy when we sat down to eat. In fact, I remained a little speechless as they succumbed to each others humor. But soon I realized that there was nothing of which to despair. My thirst and hunger quickly abated and I began to join in on their parodies and mirth. Following the salmon, rice, and salad I brewed some strong coffee for Jonathan and myself while the girls took a nap.

Meanwhile we resumed discussing *The Mangroves* in my study. I took out the old manuscript left in the cupboard and apprised him of the ghostly presence the girls and I had experienced. Then I revealed to him my latest and most modest creation, a story that I had begun in the tropics about these apparitions. Different from my other writings this one possessed humor and he was pleased with this turn of events. It, I suppose, was in part more palatable than my other books fraught with tragedy and disillusionment, as they were. He was particularly pleased with my words about the angry succubus that haunted our halls and the dog barking at seemingly nothing.

With these curiosities I had insulted and beaten back these disembodied spirits. Together we began to crown these celestial bodies with mere chance remarks planning the incarceration of these imps with every word. Moreover, though their permanence was undeniable their preoccupations could best be effaced by giving them a name and calling them down. Yes, we had concocted a game that would rob them of their efficacy, cutting their

141

capers with our own. We dabbled in this occult for a good hour and good natured we rebound from any further sorcery. These devils, it would seem, were becoming quite tame.

Anyway, perhaps because of my behavior with he and the girls, Jonathan proposed that he go to a hotel. Though I renounced this idea he was adamant. And so I left him to his own devices as he promised an early return tomorrow to complete the remainder of work.

Bright and early the next morning I awoke to the telephone. It was Chad. Apropos of his diligence he had arranged the dates, places, and times to rendezvous with his European cronies and counter parts. I smiled to myself jubilant about my prospective voyage and thanked him for his troubles. Soon Jonathan arrived and I told him about the news. Our rites of passage had been approved and we stood by the altar of my desk inwardly pleased. It was only a matter of time now before we were well on our way and we were glad for this turn of events.

Jonathan walked to the kitchen for coffee while I sat gaping at the last part of the manuscript *The Mangroves*. Again there was laughter as the day before. Apparently the gals were drinking coffee as well. I thought, to my jealous self, that there was no need to fuss but, perhaps, I was being deceived. And so to save face I crept toward the kitchen, my ears cocked up for any morsels of damaging innuendo. I couldn't make heads or tails of their banter but it was lively and jocular in nature. Someone or everyone was parading about using me as the butt of their jokes. This much was insinuated by their refrain from this silliness and the waning of their wits that, by now, had me by the collar. I hadn't put on my bathrobe yet and I was chilled to the bone. So I stood there shivering. This managed to draw hoots and hollers at my demeanor and I became more and more certain that something was conspiratorial about this arrangement. I was on the brink of my first row with the girls and Jonathan as well.

I said to Jonathan that we had a lot of work to do (which was true) and I proceeded to go to the study awaiting him with a few pointed questions about their conversation. After a significant pause he entered the study. I told him straightforward that they must be getting along quite well. And I continued on in this same vein mentioning that we never laughed so full heartedly. He was beginning to grow defensive and impatient about my observations. He remarked that I sounded resentful without cause and that there was nothing ill humored of which to speak. They were laughing at Peanuts and nothing more until I showed up looking quite comical, he said, to be perfectly frank. These remarks served to chasten me and my ill conceived accusations and, accordingly, I apologized.

The rest of the day followed without incident though there appeared to be awkward moments and expansive silences. I tried, without much success, to put a good face on it all. Nonetheless, the damage had been done and I felt a pang of guilt separating us. *The Mangroves* had been thoroughly annotated and I think we were both pleased at its outcome. We agreed that before our departure to

144

Europe I would send to him my manuscript about the ghosts.

It was settled but before he left I wished only to mend the wounds I had inflicted without due cause. So in keeping with our former status I led him to the thrift shop to say goodbye to the girls. Hugs and kisses were passed around and I chose a few self deprecatory remarks to imply my regrets. Outside, at his rental car, I apologized effusively at my behavior and I told him, flat out, how keen I was traveling abroad with him. He appeared not to think one way or another of our little scuffle and we left it alone.

That evening the girls approached me about my disposition, wondering what on earth was I thinking. I told them that I was having a difficult time sharing them and that my vulgarity was entirely without provocation. As I didn't know what else to say I excused myself after these apologies and made tracks to my haunted study.

There my concentration was deficient such that I could no longer write. Having edited *The Mangroves* had depleted my sense of direction for any new material and so fatigued and repentant I lay down my head and fell fast asleep. The dreams that came were almost without precedence. A pack of wolves, deep in the forest, were tearing me apart and my only recourse was to reach for my pen and paper that just barely lay out of reach. I awoke with a start, unable to situate myself in time and place. "Where am I," I weakly moaned. Then finally came my consciousness and the spoils of the day seemed dazzling. I longed to see Helen and Elaine but I noticed that their door was locked. My, my, I thought, they really were upset and I pledged never again to let jealousy be my partner. Tomorrow I would make things up to them, hoping it wasn't too late. For what would I do without them? They had shown me true joy for the first time in my life and not the bookish variety.

Perhaps I could mend the rift by purchasing for them another car. All we had to date was an old, spavined truck to make runs for the thrift shop and the grocery store. I was like a beaten puppy and without my master. Surely there must be a path back to their hearts. To this effect I wrote them a comical poem and made them breakfast. Later I would help them in the shop giving them the day off. Who knows, I thought, perhaps they had washed their hands of me. To imagine myself alone was tantamount to suicide. Would they be at home when I returned from overseas? Suddenly I began to think of canceling my trip. I couldn't very well subject myself to the scrutiny of my peers and antagonists alike with these idle thoughts of separation looming about.

After last yesterday's dream my study had become my cage. Meanwhile, the girls had let the dog out of the bedroom and from the silence I gathered that they had returned to sleep. My patience was getting the best of me and so I took Peanuts for a walk to the bay. Admiring the tranquil waters seemed to put both of us in a happy mood and my capacity to brow beat myself for my errors was diminishing.

When we returned Helen and Elaine had finally raised themselves from the bed, had read the poem, and were sipping coffee upon the patio. Approaching them through the back gate we all, of

147

a sudden, broke into laughter and, of course, Peanuts was wagging his tail. I told tem that before they were simply blinded to my faults and vices, and that I would shape up. That was enough said. We entered the house and played some music with which to dance. Then they led me to the bedroom to show me, I suppose, what I was missing last night. Afterwards I cringed at the absurdity of the querulous actions of which I had been guilty. We spent the day rummaging through belongings that had been left the night before. Though the girls and I were reaping the benefits of royalties from the last few novels we maintained our frugal habits and accordingly they began to pick out clothes for my trip.

The last days of the month passed by, each day more momentous with pleasure than the last. My writing about the ghosts entitled *The Ghouls* had been consummated and sent to Jonathan and my belongings were packed. I was good to go! Jonathan had taken a flight closer to his home and we were to meet in some odd fifteen hours. I hugged and kissed the gals, not without a tear, and I soared off into the blue skies.

VII

From the moment that I mounted the stairs from the metro I had taken from the airport I was exuberant beyond measure. I wished that Helen and Elaine could be here with me. It all served to remind me of how quickly my life had changed these past years. I was presently back in the shoes of my itinerant self. However, I was a wanderer with a home and playing the part of the artist in foreign lands. Something of a celebrity, I was being paid for these travels and spreading the good word about my several novels.

Upon this night my heart quickened at the sight of the restaurants and all the people milling about. But soon, all too soon, I would be pummeled with questions about myself that seemed so very personal. Moreover, their words and deeds would cut deeply into me. That much I knew. "No, I must lie at critical times," I told myself. For

149

never so much as noble I would otherwise be led by the scruff of the neck toward these trials, experiencing crime in the air, and without exoneration. What was the fuss about this chain of words, what was the fuss, indeed? I had risen from the ranks of the homeless to my newborn self with all my flaws, defects, and spiritual disfigurement and I was still the toad of this loathsomeness.

Anyway, no need to sweat this thing out. Time would pass one way or another. The weather would pass one way or another. As long as I was visited by my muse I should no longer object. I must drive this nail home not giving any credence to the nonsense they might impart. Yes, I have become engaged in this twaddle without recourse. It is, after all, a business like any other, I suppose. Either it is good bread or bad bread and nothing else seems fitting. So I must persevere with resolve and magnanimity. Though it would sometimes seem that my brain was addled and I might take umbrage I was as forgiving as the next man. So these wounds shall mend. Enough of dreams! "They will only beget slivers and specks wherever I go," I mused. Sometimes flippant with my remarks I will endure, to the best of my ability, as they say.

Yes, once upon a dream I had been sundered by heartache but now the music is clear and mellifluous and I am at my beloved Paris.

I met Jonathan at the agreed place of rendezvous, the metro stop at Place Monge. There stood the hotel at which I had stayed as a young man. We installed ourselves and our belongings but as neither of us could sleep we took to the streets. Jonathan spoke French fluently while I only knew an impoverished variety. He showed me to one of his favorite bars where we indulged ourselves late into the night. Back at the hotel we had a nightcap of cognac with the friendly concierge. Then we both retired to our room. As it was a decent hour at home I telephoned the girls to tell them of my arrival and exhilaration, and to note that I had met up with Jonathan. They wanted to hear all about it but as it was late and I was feeling fatigued I dismissed myself prematurely telling them I had an early appointment.

We awoke at the same time still antsy from the day before and partook of some coffee at a nearby café. Together we studied a few of the possible questions that might arise during my interview. From *Tyranny and the Devil* to my latest and eighth book *The Mangroves* we reviewed the texts and what was most distinguishable among them. I hadn't read the first one for some time now and I found myself groping in the darkness here and there. But equally I discovered some of it to be crisp in memory. It was our guess that from the sale of the books in France that *Tyranny and the Devil* would most likely serve as a fulcrum to the others. This suited me well as it being my first novel I had a fondness that rose above the others. It was my namesake, so to speak. Nevertheless, as time approached I was finding it difficult to catch my breath. If I failed miserably it would all seem like an enormous and bitter mistake. In this regard Jonathan came to my rescue, putting me at ease and telling me not to make much of it.

At the station I met with the interviewer and I was relieved to hear his accolades for my work. He didn't appear at all to be the shark that I was expecting. Of course, with the autobiographical nature of most of my writings, it was difficult to attack me without damning me personally. It was settled. If I felt the question to be without merit I would resort to humor and flippancy and, on the sly, diminish the import of the interview. After all, I wasn't entirely without any resources. No, I had a few jests up my sleeve. Something to take the edge off. What was my task but to entertain? To and fro we would wander through the labyrinth of words telling tall tales of my past, present, and future. As the interview progressed I could see that there was no need to be sore from the outset. Why should I spoil the conversation, expecting insolence on the part of the host, I queried. No, we had transcended poor manners for domestic and, sometimes, prosaic questions. Accordingly I found myself warming to the situation without the least objection. Quite the contrary, I wasn't afraid to poke fun at some of the more desperate circumstances and I could see a certain reciprocity taking place without clammy hands. Upon the conclusion my

153

dear host congratulated me on my work and acumen. I saluted him in return telling him of the great ease in which he had ensconced these proceedings. A tremendous relief followed and as I left I could feel that tears were in my eyes.

Jonathan sensed the host and his tenderness and rallied toward my cause claiming a victory of the first interview and an example of those to follow. We were both hungry and Jonathan had procured the directions to a restaurant nearby from one of the sound crew. We ate enough for four people and had a glass of wine to celebrate my triumph. Later we would move across town to a similar arrangement, one that would hopefully provide the same nurture as the last.

What, with the jet lag and the wine, we decided to return to the hotel to take a nap. We left a message at the front desk to awaken us in two hours time and marched upstairs. I awoke at the sound of the telephone and felt a little groggy and irritable at the demands of the interview.

At the next station I was put off by the haste with which they received me and I felt myself fumbling with words and proving myself to be inadequate of their expectations. I looked down only to see Jonathan as he thumbed his nose at me. Suddenly I was laughing to beat hell. He had fractured the self importance of the interview with this gesture and I abruptly came into my own shaking off any doldrums of the day. Yes, with a few well chosen words I would beat these others back and retrieve any lost dignity they may have incurred.

Hours later, at the bookstore, I signed my books and enjoyed the freedom of being without much of an audience. However, I found myself mumbling and began to worry about my condition with the stress of the interview that had almost broken me. There was only a thin membrane that presently protected me from my so-called illness and I wondered how I might persist in this climate. It seemed like only a matter of time before I had my 'fall from the world' and I wished for the first time that I hadn't come. I sought, but in vain, for something that might mute the terms of this struggle. I truly thought that I was over this calamity but I had been proven wrong. When I had toured the states I was less daunted than here in a foreign land. Perhaps because here I had presupposed an inveterate misunderstanding not speaking French myself.

My mind began to soar like a freak. Voices began to summon me forth. Add to this displeasure the tendonitis in my left Achilles and you had me mumbling to myself while I hobbled. Was someone trying to disable me from my duties? I winced as I endured these various pains cursing the voices, muttering to myself as I drifted into the crowd. Outside I had been struck by a blast of hot air. Trying to lose these antagonists I pressed on and as I crept one-legged by my nemesis I finally found the metro back to the hotel. I had left prematurely from the book signing to avoid this onslaught of voices and paranoia. I could have told them about my life but it wouldn't have made a difference.

I tried to lose these devils as so many times before but it was no use I couldn't tear myself away from this mob. I am bloody with this curse, I moaned. "What about these trade winds, mon frere," I muttered, rolling my eyes, my head a little cocked. It was too late. I couldn't be turned back now. Despite this turn of events I was beginning to regain my composure. I would telephone the bookstore to make amends for leaving early, apologizing profusely if need be.

Jonathan had beat me to the hotel and was sitting by the front desk. No doubt he was worried about me. Seeing him made me feel further that my mood had swung around. I told him very simply that this flock of people had me coming and going, so to speak, but that I was better, indeed, and that I was ready to resume my post at the bookstore.

Retrieving the key from the front desk I briefly opened my wallet to pay for the room in advance. Jonathan noticed the wad of cash and counseled me about the dangers of carrying so much on my person. I told him it was a new habit I had not wanting to ever again be destitute as before and that this put me at ease. However, I could see his point as I, no doubt, looked the part of the tourist and dangers always loomed about such a disposition.

In our room I telephoned the bookstore telling Ida, the manager, that I was sick to my stomach. It had something to do with travel and a big meal, I said, and she seemed understanding enough. I would return in two hours to finish the signings. As if this dark curtain had been lifted I succumbed to sleep feeling all the better for it, arising to take the bull by the horns.

As we both left Jonathan told me not to rush off as before without consulting with him first. I agreed with my apologies. He said that he only wished for my health and that no matter what followed nothing was worth losing one's faculties. Again I agreed thanking him for his watchful eyes and forgiveness.

We entered the bookstore and I began counting objects, grouping things into the number of fifteen. I once again felt like an archer, planting his feet to let go of the arrow. I found myself to be particularly astute, clever with my play of wit, and my anecdotes. That is until I met with a troubled young man who, although he didn't speak English himself, I could see that he was worked up over something I might have said. Fortunately Jonathan was there to translate. Apparently he was saying that he had written many of these same lines and that I was merely a plagiarist butting into his own creations. Furthermore he was adamant about my having seen his manuscript that had been stolen. I told him, through Jonathan, that it must be coincidence and that I wasn't aware of his writings. He only cursed at me and stomped out of the store in a mad fit.

PART THREE

I

I didn't care for the swagger of this incorrigible loon. Jonathan said as much, noting that he had cursed at me without let and I was, according to him, to watch out with some vigil. He told me in no uncertain terms to lay low and confide in nobody toward such evil eyes. He was an execration to be dealt with and I could register the alarm that Jonathan had bestowed. Perhaps he was not coming clean, fretting to worry me too much from the exact translation. No, something more lay within the confines of these insults, this mighty harangue. Should I renounce the tomb of these wanderings? I thought to myself. Should I return home prematurely to claim my lost loves? Oh, but for now I must shine. He was only a mere aberration and for goodness sakes this was Paris, my lost love. Within her arms I was reaching new heights and depths.

We took our last day visiting an exhibition of the Impressionists and the Rodin museum. Though it helped to placate matters my worry about exacerbating my illness had been aroused and I treaded on thin ground. Down and out, no doubt, this ragged man, whose meaning eluded me, was still a specter raising his head. But meanwhile this philosophy of light bounding around us seemed to make us safe from such bestiality. Tomorrow we would depart for Montpellier.

Taking the train we traversed the French countryside to the south of France, to a university town. We installed ourselves in a hotel and made tracks to the school. There the shining face of an eager student blossomed. She ran the local radio station and appeared to be genuinely excited as were we. Hopefully her questions would not be too painful, I thought. But she was quite the contrary! She had read all of my work and was gushing with praise almost foreign to me, almost making me blush. I reciprocated telling her how pleased I was that my books had entertained her and I apologized for my French. Moreover she asked if I wouldn't mind signing a book for her. Again I felt humbled and a little embarrassed by her admiration. I had forgotten what a pleasure youth could be and made a mental note to return to such "country" universities.

But then, upon departing, it happened! The schizophrenic named David, according to Jonathan, appeared across campus. No doubt he had trailed us from Paris or had become apprised of my itinerary through a newspaper. However, what was he doing here? As we approached he raised his hand like a pistol and gestured obscenely. Then he simply vanished.

Consequently, feeling threatened, we notified the police. Nonetheless the authorities said that they couldn't very well do anything without some probable cause. Together we scowled at their imperturbable reply and hailed down a taxi to take us to the local bookstore. The tendon in my leg was still sore and I couldn't depend on myself to walk that far. The store was quite crowded and, according to the merchant, it was because of me. I felt, once again, like a celebrity. Here most of the clientele knew my name and my books perhaps better than myself. And so, despite the appearance of

David, I was having the time of my life and I made certain that the customers knew of this.

But just before closing David entered. He made no bones about it, that is, that I was nothing more than an impostor. (This Jonathan later revealed to me.) Meanwhile the crowd rallied to my cause telling him to go soak his head and such like in both French and English. Though I was grateful for their remarks I worried about his exacting revenge on others including myself and Jonathan. He finally dashed out muttering inanities and drivel, scratching himself like a monkey, and yelling loud enough to raise the dead. I responded to others that I was sorry for the intrusion but that the man was very ill. Then I felt the irony of ironies, as I was hearing faint voices myself.

I asked a few of the students where a good restaurant was nearby. Effervescent they all set to bickering about the best café in town telling us that they would gladly drive us and if it met with our approval that they would dine with us. Without a qualm we agreed and followed one of the students to their car.

163

At our table one of the girls began to flirt with me anxious, no gainsaying it, to try her hand at the nut behind the books. She was particularly eager to know if I actually slept with two women. When I told her the arrangement she sidled by me telling me quite frankly that she had slept with two men and at another time was with a woman and one man. However, when I told her that I was faithful to my women she immediately began picking Jonathan's brain and bedroom habits. At this I laughed until I wept.

To my surprise I overheard Jonathan saying that he was gay. This, again, made me laugh inwardly until I cried. In fact, what with the drinks and this youth surrounding me, I was giddier than ever. I began to wonder if Helen and Elaine somehow knew about Jonathan's sexual preference. After all they were sometimes clairvoyant in their observations. Hadn't they, more than once, read my mind? Why, of course, I presumed, that was the reason for their disgust at my jealousy. Thus I slapped myself good for believing that he was after the girls.

164

I must confess, without his editing skills, some of my books might not have seen the light of day. Yes, I owed him a great deal and I would let him know about this post haste. No, a kinder man never lived and I am nothing more than a wounded animal. Finally I calmed down, ceasing with my fit of laughter, and poured more wine for everyone while I resumed with a few well chosen anecdotes. This had the desired affects of loosening everyone's tongues and we all began to jabber at the most ludicrous objects of discourse. Claiming that everyone was insane we all adjourned to the bar to speak the language of the great ape. Enough ventured and said I caught a ride back to the hotel while Jonathan stayed on to close the bar. In spite of David the trip thus far was going quite well.

Barcelona was our next stop and as neither of us spoke Spanish I felt like we would be in for a big surprise. Disembarking from the train we both gave into our hunger and descended upon a small restaurant. It was so dark that it appeared to be gutted by flame. Here we sat wondering about David and his whereabouts. Afterwards, walking

165

by a newsstand, Jonathan picked up a French newspaper. There on the front page was a grisly story about a man who had murdered an author. It wasn't too far fetched to assume that this was David or whatever be his true name. Had he the appropriate papers and could he cross the border into Spain? And what of our report to the French police? Was the officer merely duping us? Were they using us as bait not wanting us to fear for our lives? If so where were the police in Montpellier and where were they now? We chose to go, once more, to the authorities to report David. There again we met with a very cool reception and stormed out not wishing to explain any further.

We entered a modest hotel and checked into the front desk. People appeared rude, particularly the police on the streets, and I was more than a little frightened about getting sick in this cauldron of morbidity. In fact we both couldn't wait to dash out of sight, saving any impetus for the interviewing host.

I awoke from my nap trembling from a sordid dream of chase and murder. My nerves were on edge as was Jonathan's and we agreed not to be separated in case of David's reemergence. If this apparition materialized we would most likely have to do battle. If not we would be lending him the advantage of assailing us on his own time and terms. Thus we left vigilant and circumspect, on our toes about this reprobate. Still we were feeling more and more the foreigner and less safe than in France. At the police station we both felt that we were being victimized rather than helped. We had pleaded with them to see reason but without success. Apparently there were many such characters and they couldn't be bothered with our case of circumstances.

At the radio station, once more, we met with the interviewer. I wasn't certain if it was my wandering eyes and lack of attention or if the host was being surly. Matters seemed to be going from bad to worse. He seemed to be preoccupied with the crudest form of churlishness. I became increasingly aware of this dogged presence nudging me uncomfortably along through his fatuous observations and I cringed in these close quarters ready to hop

167

the next train to Perugia, Italy. It was another university town where I might find amicable friends as in Montpellier. Nevertheless it was paramount that I attend two book signings before my departure. Would David reappear? With his dungeon manners he would, no doubt, become caught in his own web. He had the sensibilities of a mortician and he probably wasn't afraid of spilling a little blood on his merry way. Who was the author he had presumably murdered? Was he a foreigner as was I and did he write about madness? The police were not able or didn't wish to enlighten us on the subject and we no longer held them with any esteem. But that there was a manhunt for this devil was our sole conclusion.

As the bookstore was almost entirely without patrons I poured myself a cup of coffee and sat to read one of my favorite authors. I realized from a flyer upon the door my name and a time announcing my presence. The time, I noticed, was an hour latter than my arrival. Surely a small crowd must form for according to my publisher my name was well known in Barcelona. I had the distinct presentiment that few would show. However my impressions weren't justified as the flock began to grow. As pleasant as this was the manager delivered a rather disturbing note. It came from David who had merely wished me, tongue in cheek, good tidings until Italy. Yes, he had studied my itinerary from the very beginning it would seem. The membrane about me had come to burst and with it arrived Jonathan. No worse for wear and tear he still seemed a little aggravated after my mention to him about the note. If necessary we agreed to squander our money if it meant eluding his presence. Our private affairs were no longer private. In fact they hadn't been so since our arrival in Paris. Only now were we awakening to our desolate condition. Growing callous toward the general public we scurried to the train station to catch a lift to Perugia.

There we kept our eyes pealed for David even entertaining the possibility that he may be in disguise. After watching for quite some time I was reminded of Count Keyserling's words that many people are simply "soulless forms of behavior."

169

Wound up like automata people continued to spill in and out of the trains. Soon it would be our turn. But troubles with my mental state were surfacing. Even Jonathan looked as though he had been struck and dumbfounded. Paranoia loomed all about us. Whether it was real or imagined made no difference to our set of propositions. I didn't wish to worry him further for I could see that he was despairing himself.

I had to relieve myself and I told him that I was going to the restroom. He told me that he would, meanwhile, go to buy a French newspaper. Perhaps there might be some snippets of news about David's alleged exploits. Returning to the spot where we had earlier stood I awaited his arrival. But was this the right place, I thought, for time passed without any sign of him. My fear redoubled. Had he met with foul play? I was growing more and more nervous as the throng of people moved to and fro with great speed. Suddenly my senses seemed to open up and I found that many, if not all of this hubbub and uproar, were the police disguised. One after another I picked apart, congratulating myself for my weapons of scrutiny, laughing out loud at these forms of behavior that made no sense. Nevertheless I soon quieted down not wishing to alert David, if he be here, to this travesty. Yes, the train, no doubt, would be filled with the authorities. But where was Jonathan? What if he didn't show? I couldn't very well chase after him. If I did I might miss our rendezvous.

Our train finally arrived. There seemed to be a terrible screeching sound that presaged trouble like a collective human cry. There was a palpable sigh that issued from the public. Was Jonathan disoriented and would he climb aboard without me? Everyone was presently hobbling onto the various cars and soon we would depart. Deciding that he had probably boarded I mounted the train. Once aboard I could venture from car to car seeking him out, or so I thought. If he wasn't among them he, nonetheless, had the address in Perugia where we could once again meet. But what if he had meant with danger? The train began to rock as the departing message over the intercom faded. The haze of the light seemed to envelop me, hold-

171

ing me near in this scrimmage. I put my bag above me and took a seat. And there I sat wondering, and wondering and wondering, almost ad nauseam!

II

After my ill luck in Barcelona, Perugia suited me well. It was lit up with its terrain and plateaus but I was oppressed by Jonathan's whereabouts. My thoughts began to question where I belong, perhaps nowhere. I was merely a gypsy of the soul. It was a lonely curse. This adventure, this lease of my life has been subjected to the literati and there is no end in sight. A sad and sorry explanation, well, I have none.

I attempted to contact those that would interview me seeking out Jonathan if he had telephoned them. From the hotel at which I had installed myself I, as well, attempted to track him down but found that management were absent taking their lunch.

Nerves on edge I tramped down the boulevard figuring that I would appear unannounced to the radio station. It was about a three mile walk and it did me good to assuage the excitable and disturbed self that I was experiencing, close to madness. Losing Jonathan was a particularly ominous sign and I picked up my pace impatient to talk with the personnel about any correspondence from himself, the girls back home, my publisher, or the authorities. After brief pleasantries I broached the subject of any news from those that I knew. To my elation they immediately told me that Jonathan had called as well as my publisher. The news about his safety seemed to banish my nervous state. Apparently he had come looking for me and had missed the train. He was presently on his way and would arrive in some few hours to the radio station.

I asked the employees if anybody named David had called. After they replied "no" I told them about his previous visits and his dangerous status. Ostensibly they were not aware of the newspaper reportage nor the police but would keep a lookout for his mannerisms and intrusions.

The interview went without a hitch. In fact, with all the good news, I delighted in a show of humor. Afterwards we opened a bottle of wine and celebrated my success. They seemed genuinely interested in me and I responded by inviting them to the states for a visit. I told them about the ghosts, the women with whom I lived, the thrift store, et cetera. Then in strolled Jonathan, looking quite haggard. We embraced and introductions followed. Doubtlessly we shared in the mutual safety which was now ours. No longer expecting foul play we adjourned for a delicious repast, then returned by taxi to the hotel for a customary nap.

As had become protocol I would meet at a bookstore for a signing. Having not seen David for some time we began to dismiss any future confrontations. Perhaps we had lost him altogether or he had been arrested at the border. However, for peace of mind, we now went nowhere without one another. We thought about buying a gun but being foreigners it was an impossible situation.

Without any more vexation we marched forth absent of despair. We wouldn't that easily come to perish. At least so we both came to think after this last bout with the opposition. What's more to date we congratulated ourselves for a fine performance. Jonathan was happily surprised with my deliveries and astuteness while I was, particularly in France, pleased with his dealings and discretion for my welfare. Together we were not only buoyant now but inexhaustible. After all we had restored some dignity to these tales of sheer madness and in their wake discovered new audiences. Perhaps we had put on a good show for posterity if there was any future for my books.

The bookstore had only a few people milling about but I didn't take this too much to heart. At least there was no show of David. For this much I was thankful. I had noticed that at the entry way a picture of me and the advertisement for my appearance and book titles. Apparently my publisher had rushed this off without notifying me and the picture disturbed me a little. In it I seemed to express a sadness I no longer felt. Before closing a fair crowd gathered at my desk. There were questions and compliments and, of course, books for the

175

signing. It occurred to me that I was once such a patron and I thanked them in earnest for this show of support. My gratitude was real, not imagined, but nevertheless I was beginning to miss home. The women, the dog, and even the ghosts were my old friends. Without Jonathan on this trip, I would have folded early. I said my farewell then seized my hat, the one given to me long ago by the girls.

Together Jonathan and I treaded the same thoroughfare that I had taken earlier and began to thread our way through this labyrinth to the hotel. From all the walking I began to feel flushed and hungry and we agreed upon one of the restaurants along the way. Most of all I suffered from thirst having drank wine earlier. I quickly gulped down a pitcher of water and we ordered a heavy meal looking forward to our nap. Upon leaving, as if an omen, the bells pealed from a church down the road.

At the hotel we drank to our health and proceeded to gossip like teens about our trip apart. The sunlight was brimming through my eyes. I told him that I was sorry for missing him at the train station and he told me, jokingly, that a rap on my knuckles would suffice. Well, the philosophy of our struggle was on the mend and our strength renewed. I fell into bed, helpless in the sea of dreams. I awoke as with a fever and gaped at the closet stupidly. My reflections began to stir recalling my childhood. I didn't wish to awaken Jonathan so I quietly left for a walk outside. In spite of our earlier conversation about not separating it seemed harmless enough. After all we had, neither of us, seen nor heard from David and it was highly unlikely that he would reappear. Besides I felt the need to put things in their proper prospective. We were on the final leg of our trip. There only remained Amsterdam, then London. Underfoot the paving stones began to register in my strained tendon and I dreamed of the gals and the raptures of their love. At the nearby corner the light seemed to vanish before my eyes. The farmers market, once rife with life, was now beginning to wane and the merchants were packing up their things. I could hear a siren blow in the distance which made me quake and I returned to my room without satisfy-

177

ing my mission of dispelling the anxiety brought about from our trip. However I was set on telephoning Helen and Elaine to remedy this forlorn state. And so, gathering my thoughts, I dialed the number.

I had awoken them but, of course, they were not upset. Quite the contrary, they were jubilant. They had no idea of David and his fatal meanderings and I wasn't about to tell them. Relating such a story might cause them unnecessary worry. Instead I spoke about the lighter side of our ventures sparing them the sordid details. Why I even put Jonathan on the phone to renew his acquaintance. Their closeness no longer bothered me, doubtless because of his homosexuality. One might just as well say that the three girls were talking.

After he hung up we talked to each other until the wee hours of the morning. One could tell that he suffered from the secrecy of his sexual identity and that, above all, he was a loyal friend. I smoked a cigarette and finally said good night.

Morning found us scrounging to pack our bags. At the train station we booked a car to Amsterdam and waited, sure of each others presence. Our eyes were still vigilant toward espying David but neither of us said anything. Despite keeping long hours awake the night before we were both vigorous and alive, anxious once again for new beginnings. In Amsterdam we would walk the canals and visit the Van Gogh Museum. We were almost safely home!

It would appear that the Netherlands was particularly kind to the mentally ill and their hospitality revealed as much. One might guess that my host was being interviewed instead of myself for he was elaborate in detail about social programs and treatments of which I had never before heard. But it was all done in good taste and I began to shine upon his questions. As an interviewer he was without equal. Yes, without rival he brought our conversation down the most pleasant of paths and afterwards we were invited to dine at his home. It would appear that, according to Jonathan, he was gay. This was no matter to me but it seemed to give Jonathan some form of complicity. Without any protest we got along famously. Together we were quite the ensemble, the schizophrenic and the literati.

As the end of the evening approached it was clear to me that Jonathan was going to spend the night. Our fears of David had diminished and so I bade them thanks and farewell. The sky was done up in ribbons of color. I entered the hotel, procured my room key, and went to bed for a well deserved snooze. The next morning at a stand-up bar I ordered coffee and a croissant. Then, as prearranged, I sauntered happily off to collect Jonathan and to depart for our final destination, London.

From the stoop I noticed that the door was ajar. Knocking loudly I called their names and entered. As I approached the bedroom it was as quiet as it could possibly be. I knocked once more at the bedroom door and reluctantly entered. All at once it struck me, still bodies in pools of blood. It appeared that their throats had been slit from ear to ear! I needed to see no more. I went to the telephone and with shaking hands dialed the operator. I had retrieved the address from mail on the table and proceeded to tell the authorities that we needed the police and an ambulance. With my screams there amassed a few of the neighbors wondering what the trouble was. The police arrived soon after and I led them to the bedroom. I told them about David and his idle threats as well as about his appearance in the French newspaper having killed an author. They began to sift for clues and asked me a battery of questions. I asked them in return about how he had eluded the cordon of the police. They told me that it was sometimes true that there was nothing so cunning or desperate or daring as the incurability of a criminal. I gave to them the name of my hotel as well as my passport and I was left alone for the time being. In the near future I would have to arrange for Jonathan's body to be sent home. I didn't know that much about him but the city of his mother's home. I called Chad with the bad news and I tried to pick up my thoughts from dwelling on that fatal image that was stuck in my mind. I told him that soon I must flee this land of canals, canals that before had been called the circle of hell. And to this I added that, of course, I would reject any future interviews. Yes, I would fly directly home and what's more my writing career was over. This was my last hurrah. Inspiration would no longer befriend me.

Two days had passed before the police contacted me. I was still not absolutely free to go my own way and I began to drink heavily to ease the pain. It was the only way to snuff out these reappearing symptoms. Who knows, I thought, perhaps they were assembling a case against me. But as they related that I should watch my backside and that I wasn't taken into custody I dismissed such a scenario of any merit. In fact I bought a hunting knife to protect me in case of any future confrontation and without any objection from the police.

At the bar I mumbled "The cream of the crop, the snow on the ground, the last pigeon standing." "Jabberwocky and gibberish!" I proclaimed, sinking deeper and deeper into this mire and unavoidable trap. Toasting tragedy after tragedy in my life I continued drinking until I was numb. I felt great relief that I would no longer dress things in writing, that I was free from this chain of words. Helen and Elaine were my only refuge and soon I would be in their midst. I had decided not to convey the story of Jonathan until we met in person. I continued drinking and the bartender was beginning to give me a quizzical eye. Soon I would have to dismiss myself to another bar. There was no shortage of these. They lay at every corner.

Next I entered the bar Heaven and Hell. It had a busier clientele and once I nearly laughed, to myself of course. I began to get cocky telling myself that I must search this world over for my prey, David. Perhaps I could lure him forward where I would be able to do battle. I felt that, with the gin and my incessant smoking, my heart was ready to blow. Nevertheless I continued on in this same vein not wishing to return to my room.

Through my jacket I felt my knife pleased with its presence. Underfoot the paving stones began, again, to exacerbate my tendonitis. Would everyone think that I was hobbling from drunkenness or did they really care? There was no dearth of the public now. It was the time for hideous reckoning. Everyone seemed to be drowning. So I

183

proposed to myself to visit the police station tomorrow demanding that they return my passport and let me go on my way. I had drank myself sober and without a qualm I took to my hotel ever so vigilant to my surroundings.

III

Successful at the police station I boarded the train to Calais. There I would take a boat across the English Channel to Dover and, finally, a bus to London. I was anxious to be home but not being safe as yet I didn't choose to dwell upon it. There were many miles to traverse before I would reach a clearing. It dawned on me that all my life I had played the fool and presently I was merely a seedy old man without a country. But soon, I proposed, I would no longer be a wanderer. I would become as domestic as they come. I would dig deeper and plant myself in the midst of life. Unfaltering I would make the most of these timely hours never again abdicating to success or money. We would, together, lead a modest life with immodest happiness. We would live happily ever after.

On the boat everyone collected together to avoid the hard rain. It was a dark and starless night. Eying the general public I saw no likeness to David. On a whim I ventured out on deck. Nobody was there but I felt as if I was not alone. I moved toward the parapet and there, out of the corner of my eye, I saw a gathering of darkness. It was a man with a beard but whose stature was that of David. I caught the glint from the blade and swiftly moved to the side. There, off his balance, I pushed his unsteady self over the edge. I stepped back looking about me for the presence of others. There were none. And so with the utmost secrecy I picked up his knife and along with my own I hurled them overboard. With the frigid and turbulent waters and the rain I figured that David would not last an hour. The darkness and the rain would swallow him up.

Back inside the hull of the boat I was shivering, not so much from the cold and damp, but from nerves from the altercation. At the same time I felt tremendous relief from David's demise. However I worried unnecessarily if he had truly met his mortal fate or would somehow survive. Before he had seemed so invincible whereas now there was a deep silence in myself and my secret. I still couldn't elude my memories of Jonathan and his lover, Kipp, their throats slashed almost simultaneously. This only helped absolve me of any wrongdoing. David was, after all, the slayer of who knows how many. There was justice in my self defense and I wouldn't have anymore prattle about my actions and his death.

On land, at Dover, I boarded the bus. I began to feel exuberant about all matters of things. There was a joyous calm surging through me unlike anything before. In fact my survival through sheer instinct had given me new life, an abundance of life.

Arriving in London I took to the streets quite excitable. Indeed, I was on the edge of a red letter day. And so I tramped downtown, oblivious to the world. When I examined it further it seemed as though the general public was welcoming me. I could still hear David's inhuman cry at my shoulders but this didn't deter me at all. I didn't owe him spit.

I checked into a hotel. This time there was no expense spared. Though it was late I wasn't the least bit tired. Again I took to the streets. Walking up the Thames I puffed on a cigarette on the brink of waving to my coterie and cohorts. Then I disappeared into a pub to truncate this excitability in my limbs. Nonetheless, after a few drinks I was still flying high and I began soaring with my madness almost crying out. Off to Travalger Square I went hobbling with my tendonitis and muttering strange enchantments to these many allies at my side. Soon the pubs would be closing but I couldn't very well return to the hotel. I couldn't be left alone! I entered another pub. For the small crowd there I bought a few rounds. I was still floating when they closed the doors. I almost wanted to tell them that I had a secret, a bold and heroic and immodest secret. But instead I only smiled, wishing them good tidings.

Returning toward the hotel, the Prince, I began to lose myself and my sense of direction. Few-

187

er people were on the streets. I felt as though I was being abandoned by all of these do-gooders and began cursing my fate. My tendonitis was getting worse and I now longed to be back at my hotel. At a corner I asked a few people for directions. Walking lamely with blood shot eyes I must have looked frightful. Nevertheless with due politeness they mapped out a simple course which to follow and thanking them profusely I limped along my merry way. Speaking to them, though briefly, seemed to give me back my soundness of mind. Other than ordering drinks I realized that I hadn't spoken to anybody during the entire and tempestuous day.

A strange and alien thought crept into me. What if I attended one last book signing? It would be my last and Jonathan might have urged me to do so if he was still alive. To add to this it would not be as demanding as an interview and it might help me to get back on my feet. Soon I would be home with the women and the best friends of my life. It was time to acclimate myself in this direction. I was still being hounded by these mental surges and if I wasn't careful I might confess to my so-called crime. But, I insisted to myself, it was not a crime for it was no fault of my own. It was merely an act of self defense. Surely everyone would be able to see this, that there was no recourse, and surely they would never find David. If they did they wouldn't be able to link me with it by any means. He was simply an outlaw who had met his match. Yes, I concurred, I must throw myself back into my work one last time. I must rid myself of these injustices of guilt, crime, and destiny. I must purge this helplessness and the seeking of forgiveness.

At the hotel I continued to suffer from insomnia. I couldn't do as much as close my eyes without great effort. At dawn I dressed myself and, with an uneven gait, lumbered downstairs and out the door to a nearby restaurant. Without hunger I ordered only coffee and perused the newspaper for any report on finding David. There was no such news and before I knew it I had haled a taxi to visit the bookstore. As it hadn't yet opened I shuffled around the adjacent streets. Hours later there was a good crowd and before long I was signing with a

189

crabbed hand.   With the lack of sleep I felt as though I was recovering from anesthesia.   I couldn't wait to dash out of sight.

Thus the day had ended without too much toil or worry and there was a clear path home arranged for me by Chad weeks ago. It seemed as though I hadn't seen the girls for ages. The world had since foundered before me. However I wasn't plunged into the desperation of yesterday and I still had my wits about me.

I bade them all farewell and headed for the nearest pub for some refuge to these wounds. The day was beginning to shine a little warmer inside myself even though there was nothing but clouds and rain with which to celebrate. I was but a wolf in the wilderness of the streets and asphalt chasing after some immediate pleasure. So be it, I thought. Tomorrow will come with a well deserved respite from these horrors. Once again I feel very capable, capable enough to arouse instinct and survivability despite the circumstances.

I chased down the streets in my great solitude both praising and cursing alike all by my side. But

I wasn't visible in my struggle to name this cross of mine to any other no matter the pangs that I would endure. Had we met before I might very well have befriended one and all but, no, today is different. I feel it in my bones. This is no time to waste my breath and I remain stupefied by those around me. Why should I pretend to be someone else? No, I would never incarnate a diminished soul. I may cry out but not without a reply of my own. Turn right, turn left, what is the difference between such choices? Oh, but it is perhaps a matter of life and death and we puzzle through this choice day after day. What had led me to meet the girls or my publishing house, or Jonathan's demise? All were decisions wading in futurity that was precisely mine. Fate and destiny, no sticks or stones, we have come full circle.

In my youth prospects enlightened me. It was a new world, a world devoid of any helplessness and I took it in stride. In the palms of my hands lay only riches with which to survive. In my palms lay rivers and the sea marking out my time. But presently I shall take to the skies crooning the loves of my life. In the morning the song of sparrows shall awaken me. Filled with remembrance I will descend the steps to the thrift shop. I will no longer cry out the hero or coward that I have been. There will be no more hard wintry climes and the grasses will grow as summertime grows. Peanuts and I will have our rewarding walks through the chaparral and without a haunted study the thrift shop will be my part time residence. Never again to shelve books, never again to write.

Today I walk these streets knowing I shall never return. I am haggard from loss of sleep. Back at the hotel I toss and turn, my voices are presently upon me. I cannot distinguish a distant radio from these utterances. I am used up and I feel like screaming to the world, "Enough!" But I must hang on for tomorrow I will be reunited with my true love and happiness. I push myself to go outside. There lies enormous queues of people rushing around like automata. At the Thames I feel like hurling myself in the dirty water and I am reminded of David and the English Channel. Bleak with weather, bleak with hope I carry on. I sit upon a park bench while a policeman passes and nods to me. I wonder if he knows who I am or what I have done. Nevertheless he continues on his way seemingly oblivious to my concerns.

I return to my hotel, my head hanging, a beaten man. Hungry and tired I fall fast asleep, but only for a couple of hours. When I awake it is nine o'clock. I wash my face and head out the door for something to eat. There I lounge, alone as usual. I am sent to dreaming now ready to jump out of my skin. "Tomorrow," I say to myself, 'Tomorrow!" To further combat this insomnia I attend a pub once again. I am beginning to cheer up but I am still sick in body and soul. I can now barely walk and these murmurings are omnipresent. I am chanting under my breath while they wreak confusion. My paranoia, if it is such, is surging through my vessels. Everyone appears to be collaborating for or against me. There is no gainsaying it, there is something dreadfully wrong. The reality of voices and fear is gripping me. I must flee this den for a new one making comparisons, looking for clues, and so forth and so on. I won't be an easy target.

193

No, they will have to count on a fight from me. At the next bar it is the same set up. A large group of patrons are talking about me, not to me. I am as patient as Job and occasionally I will lock onto somebody's eyes. But this is an old game and soon I tire. I must make myself presentable for tomorrow. Thus I pick myself up and shuffle back to the hotel.

The day I thought would never come is upon me. I gather my belongings and a crumpled jacket and, after checking out, I take a bus to the airport. There the atmosphere is busy but morose. Up in the sky I am giddy with anticipation. It is a long flight but it ends safely. I grab my bag overhead and disembark. Through the airport I hobble and upon exiting I spot the girls in the old truck. Peanuts sees me first and begins to bark. Then the girls rush to me and the tears begin to flow. Chad has already told them of Jonathan's end. I tell them that I am sorry and for the first time I think that perhaps it was partially my fault. Maybe down the road I will confess throwing David overboard but for now it was ours to live happily ever after. In the meantime I shall lay with my beloved in a soft hush.

Windsor, California

June 2007

www.ingramcontent.com/pod-product-compliance
Lightning Source LLC
Chambersburg PA
CBHW022106280326
41933CB00007B/274